A Collection of Mandalas

Book Two

By

Kim Jordan Blair

I would like to thank Jo-Lene Szapowal for allowing me to use her colored version of my star mandala on the cover of this book.

I would also like to thank my dear friend Renee Kritzer for allowing me to use her colored version of the square mandala on the cover of this book.

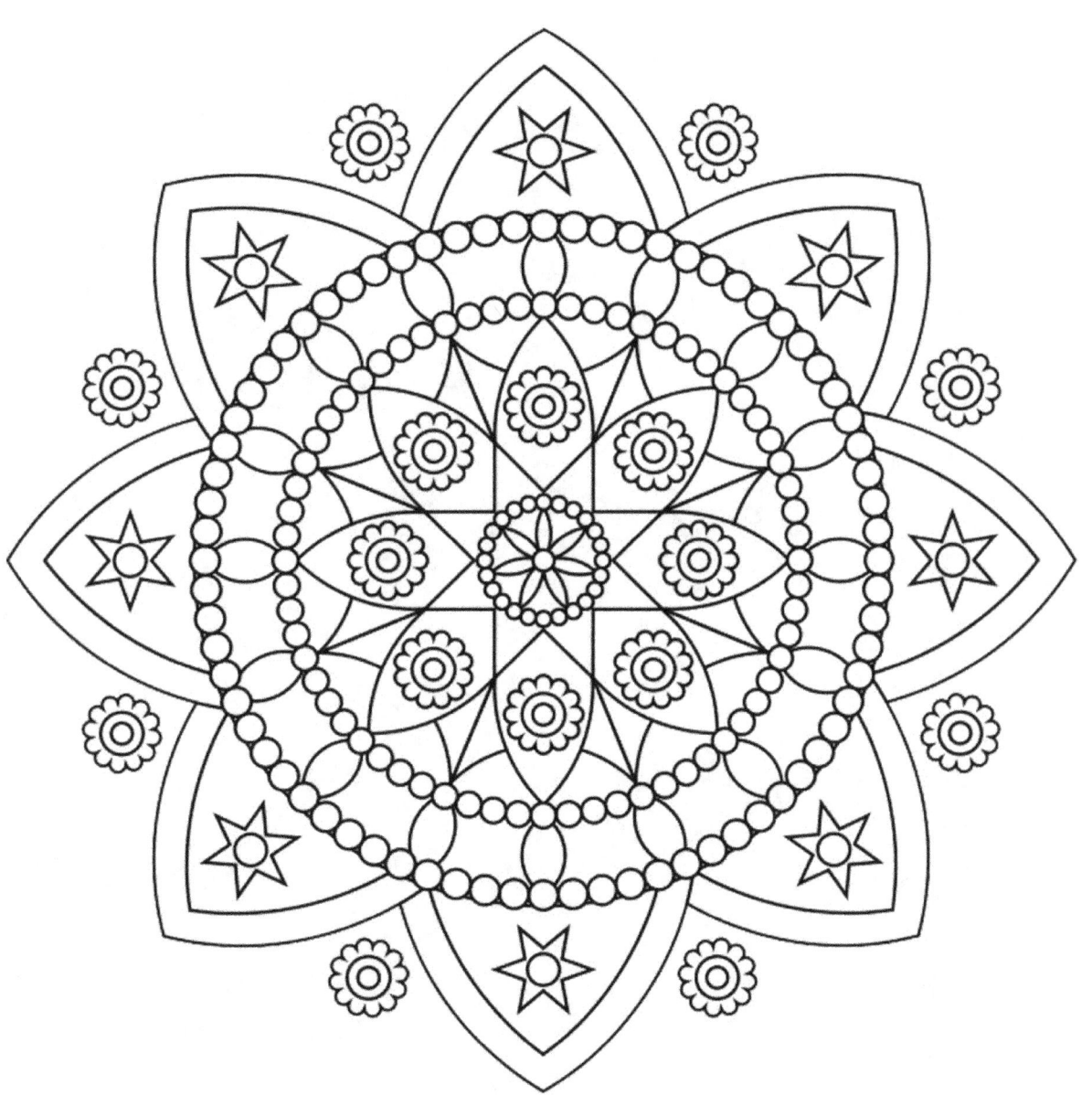

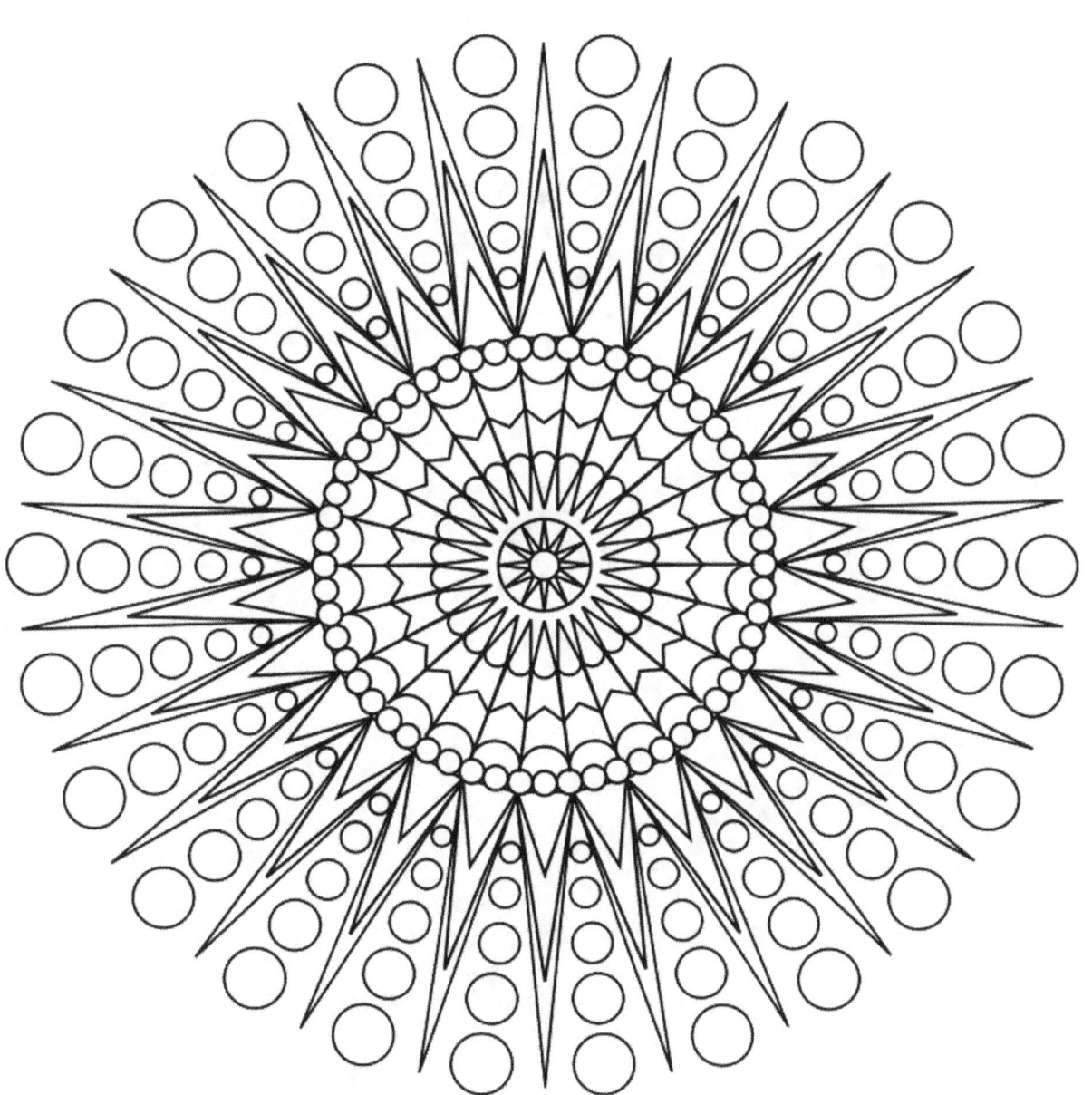

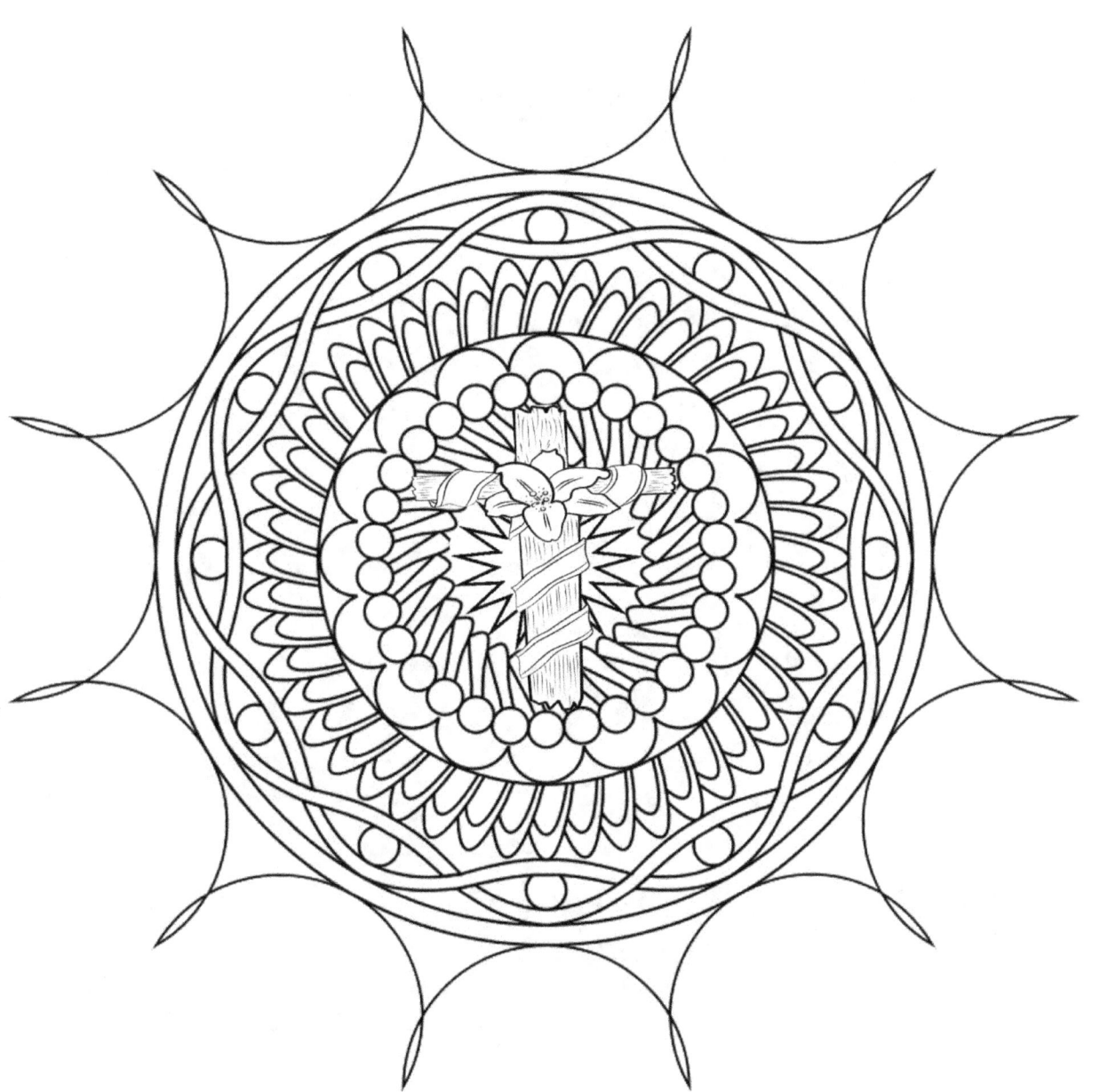

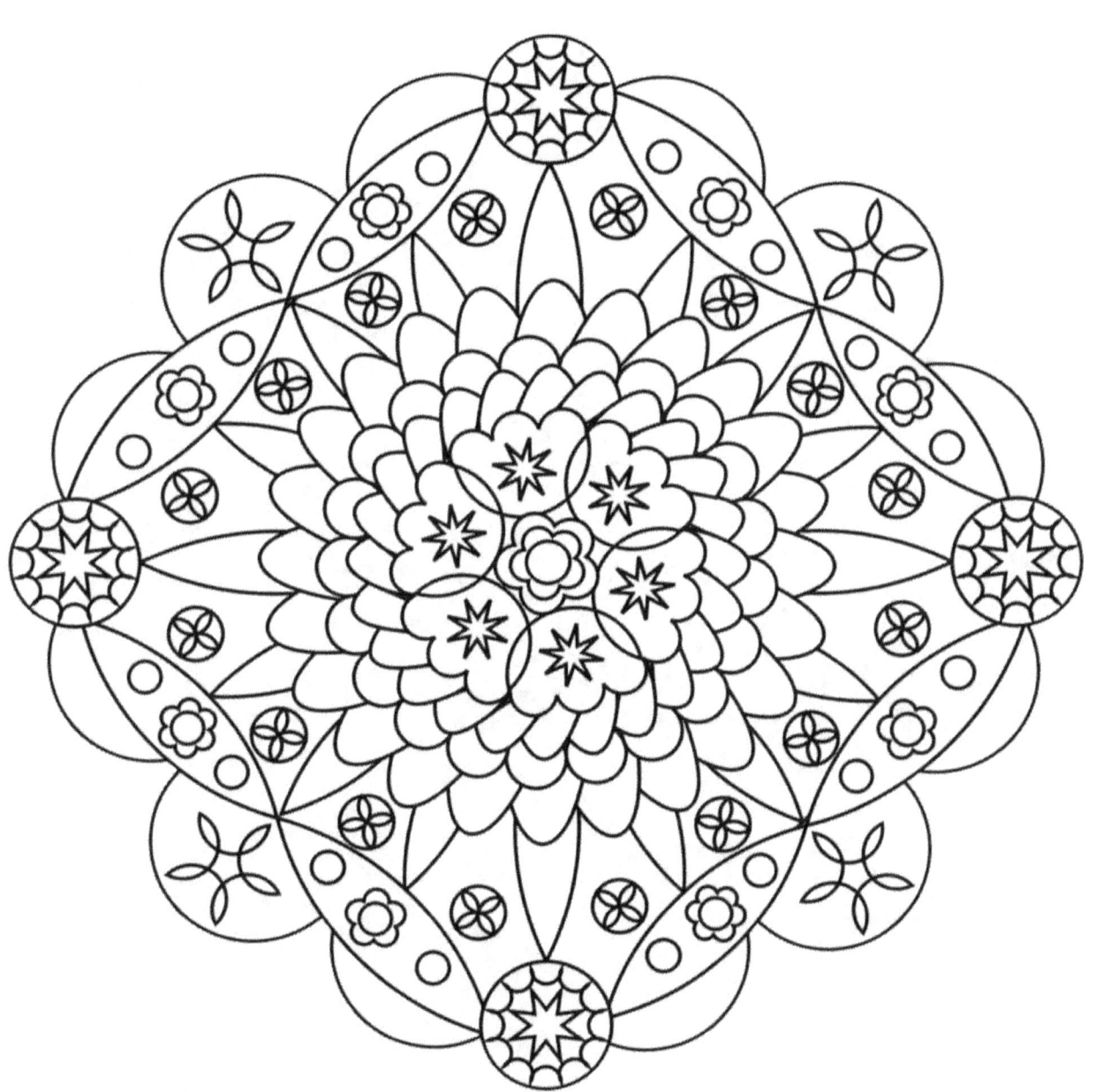

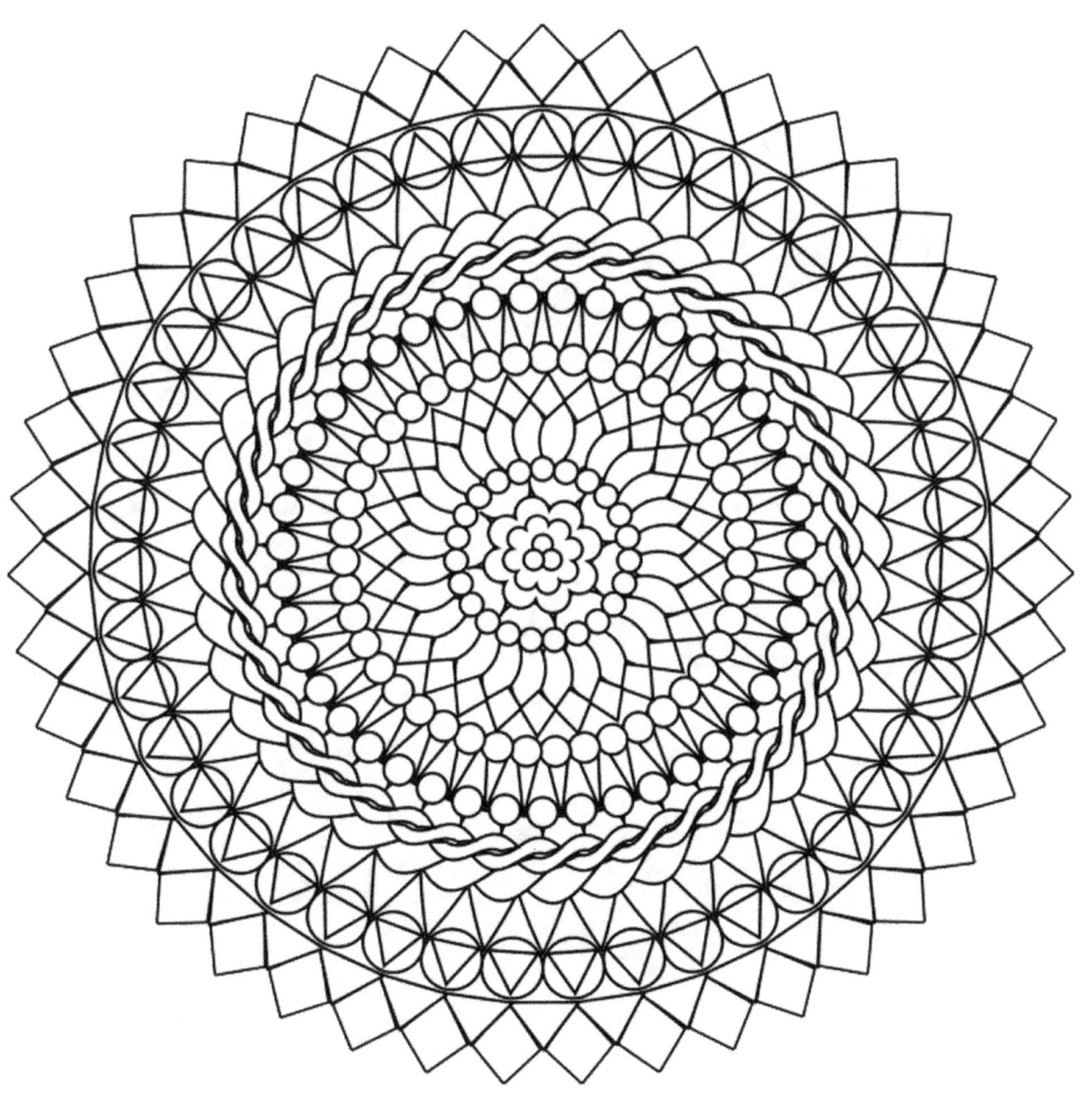

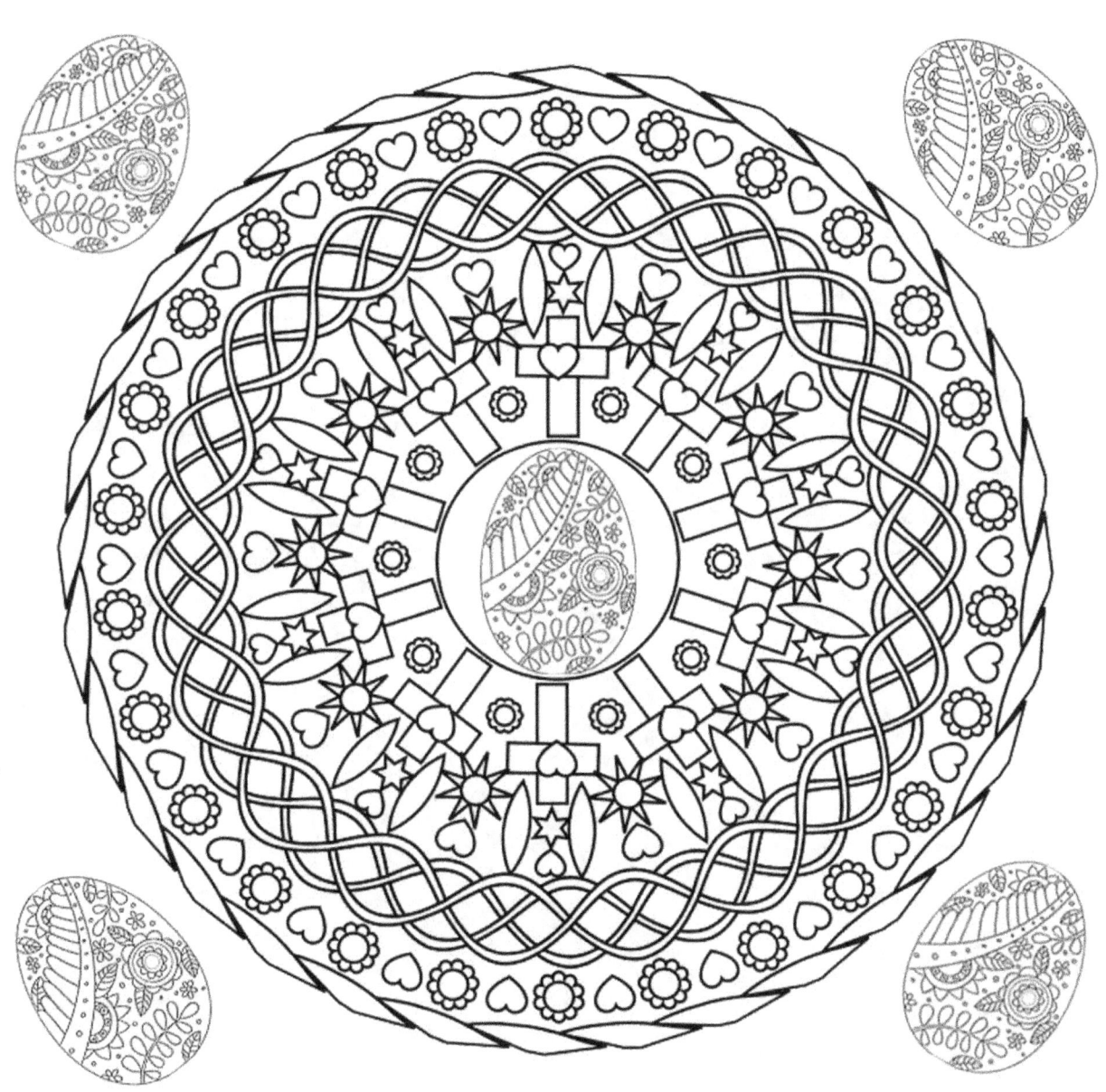

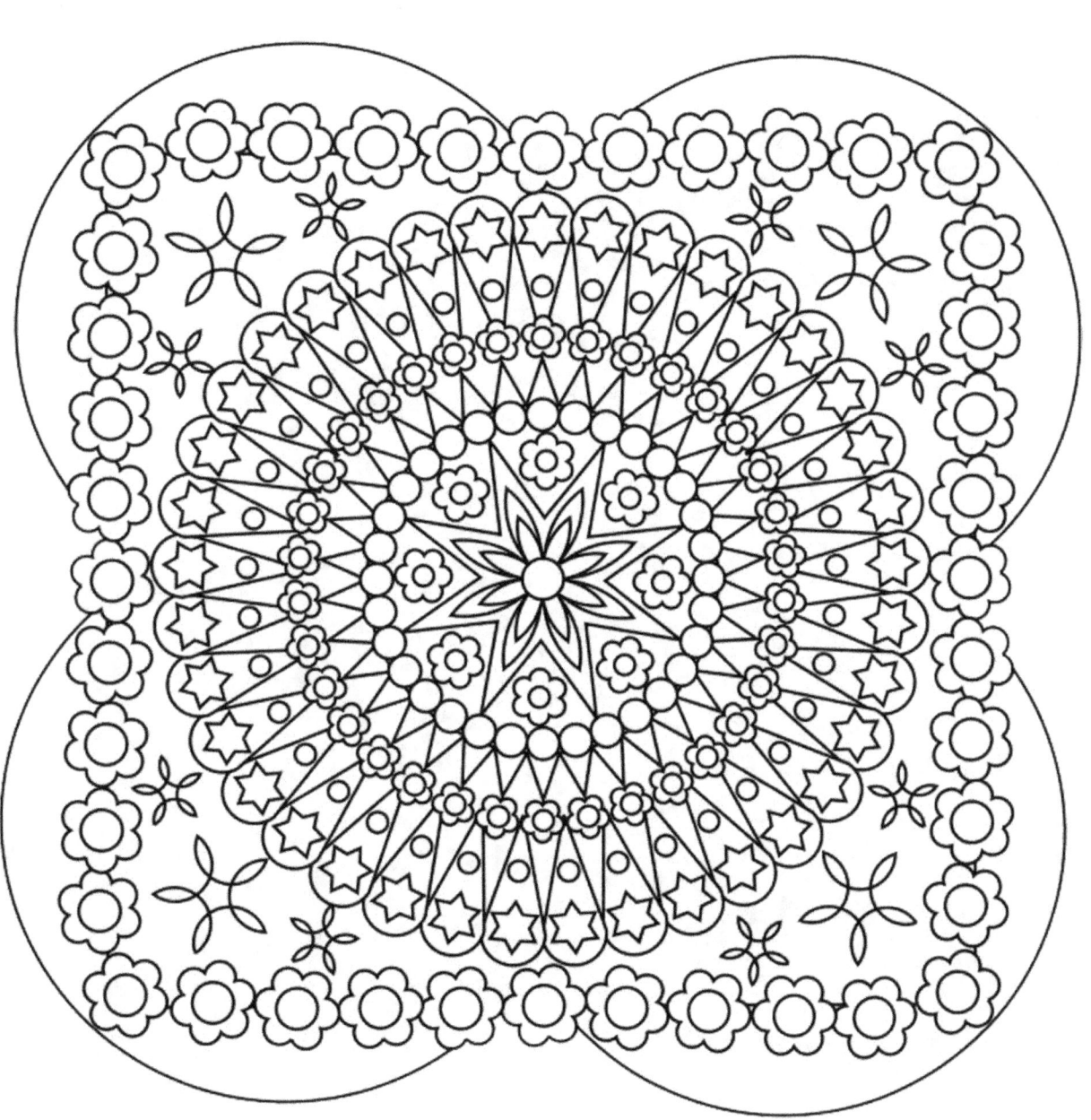

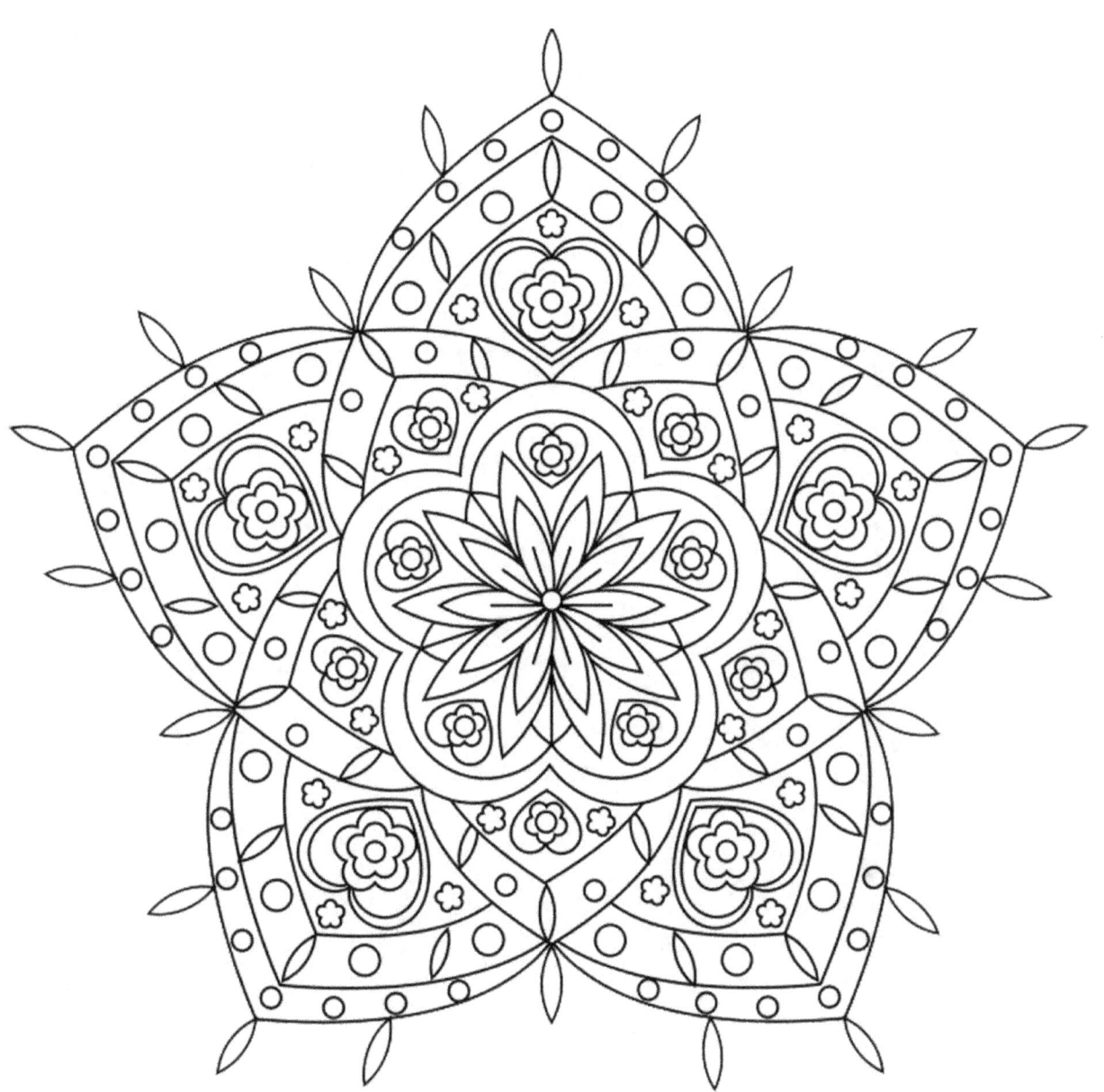

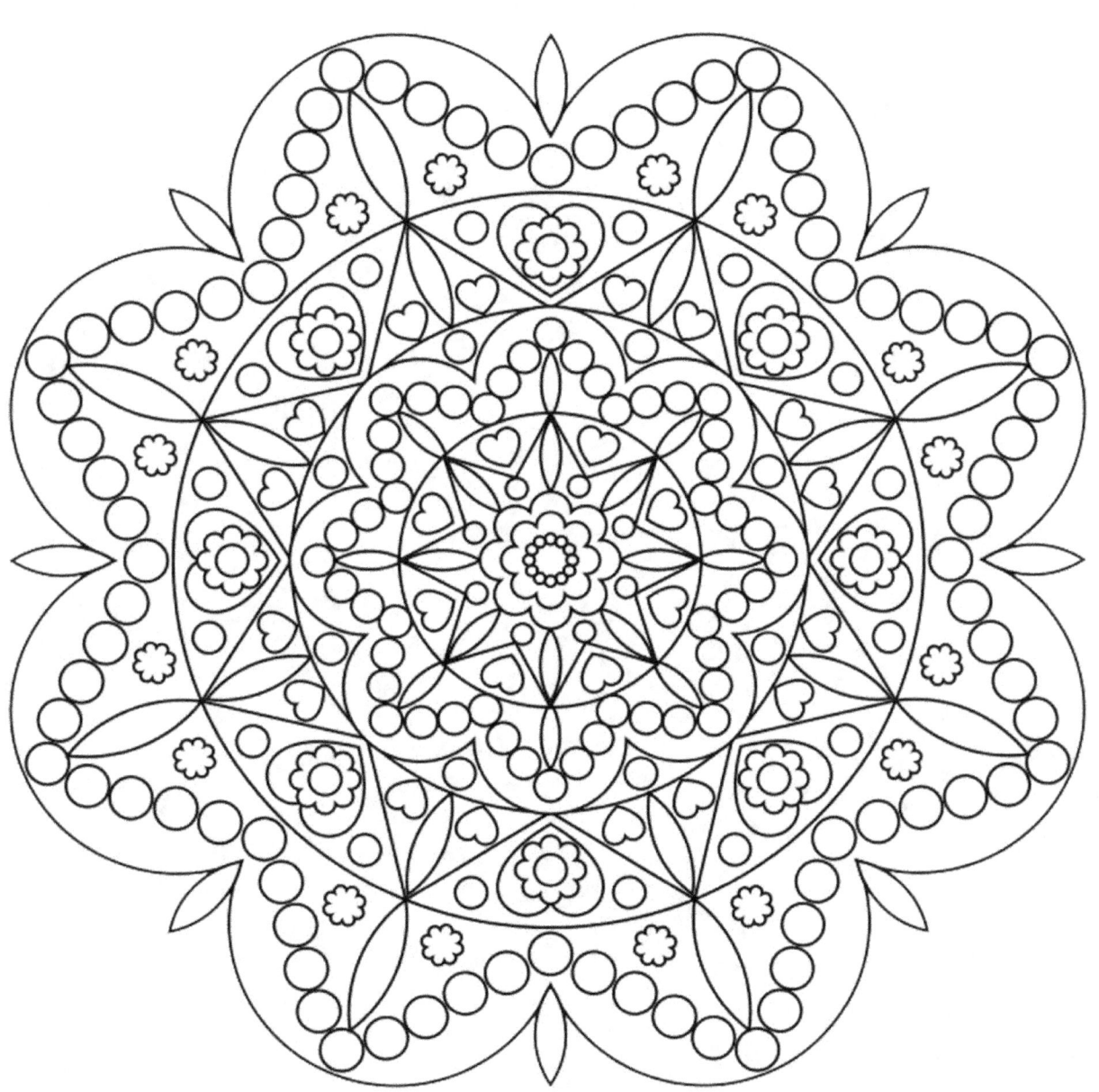

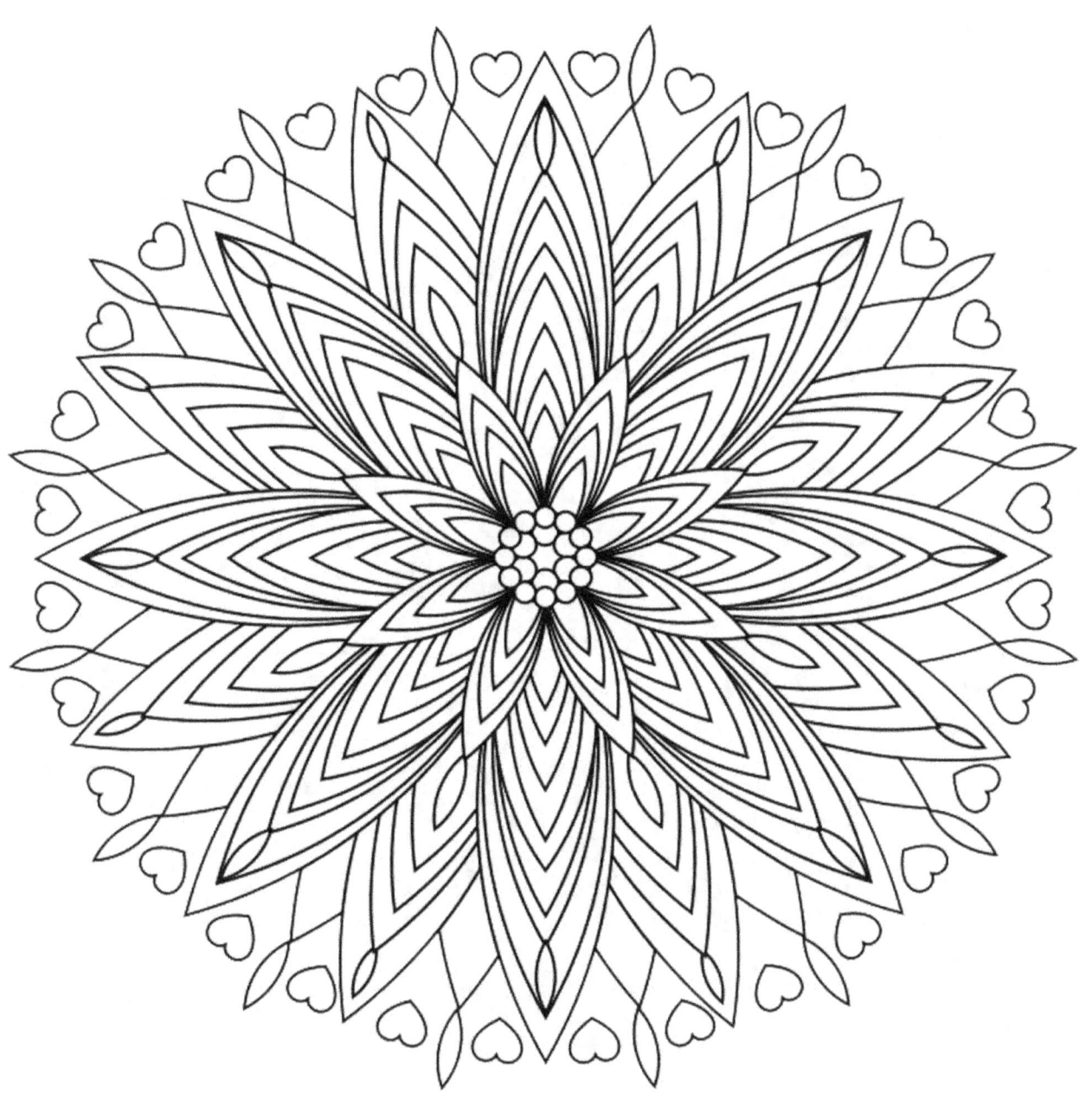

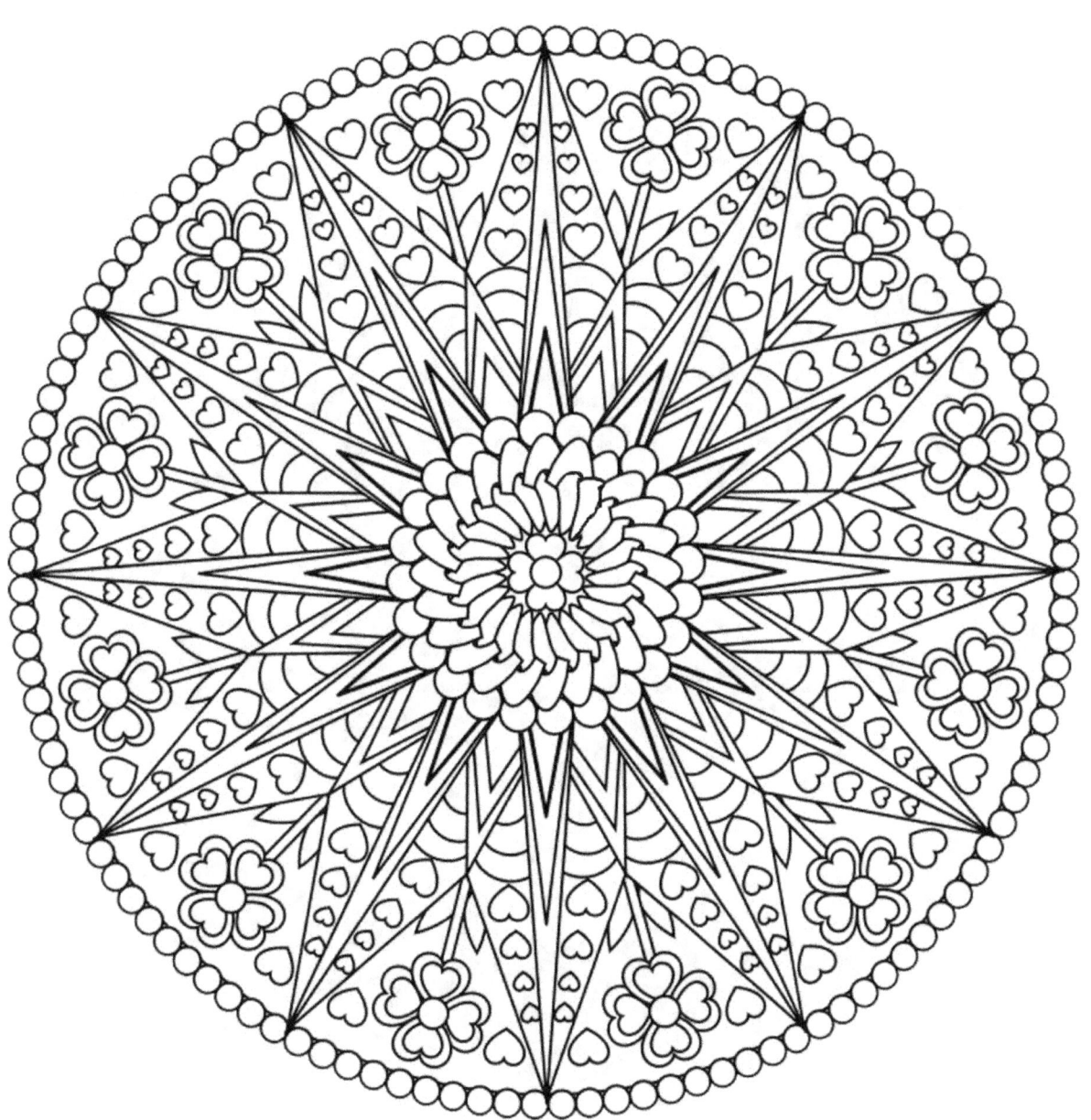

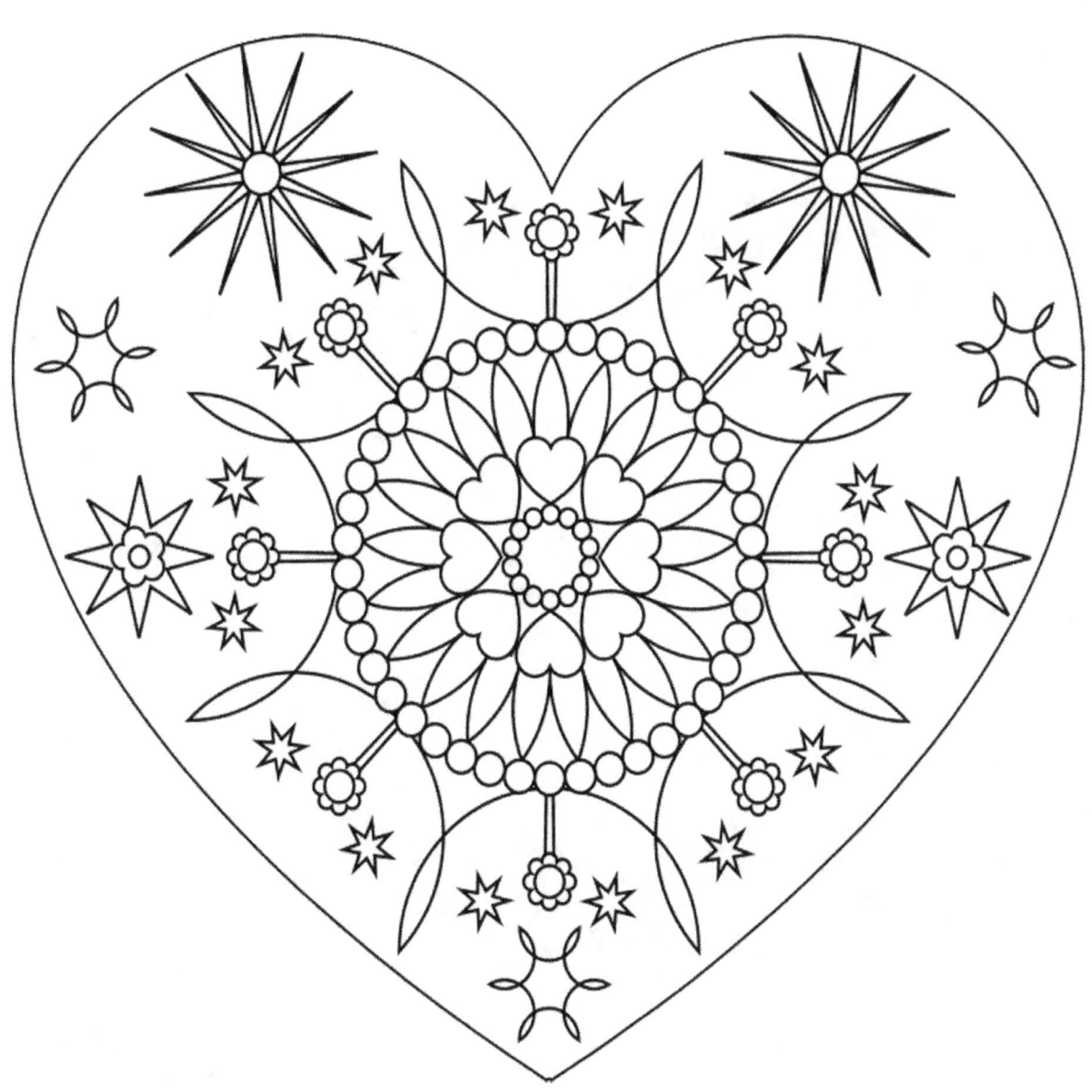

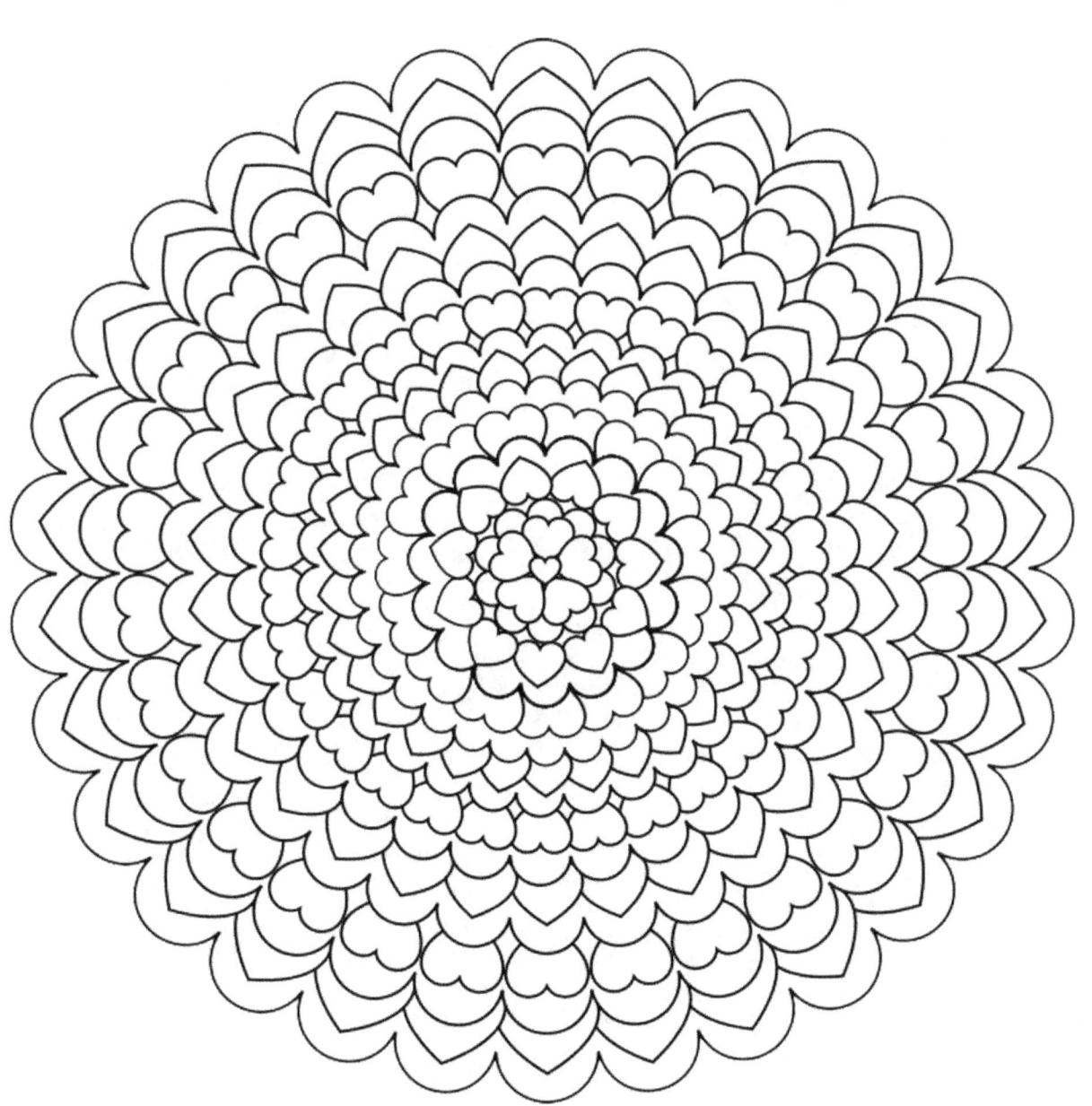

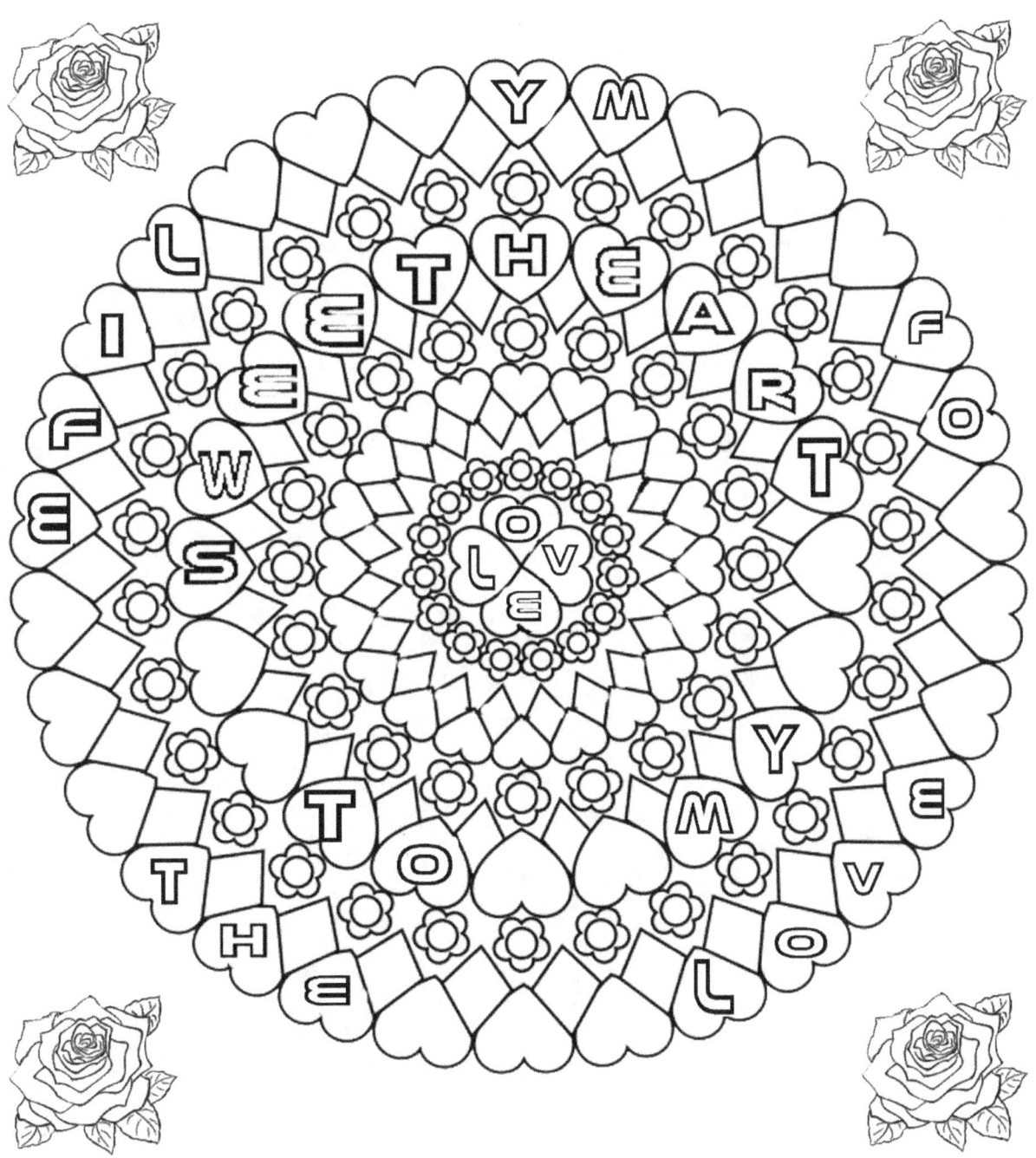

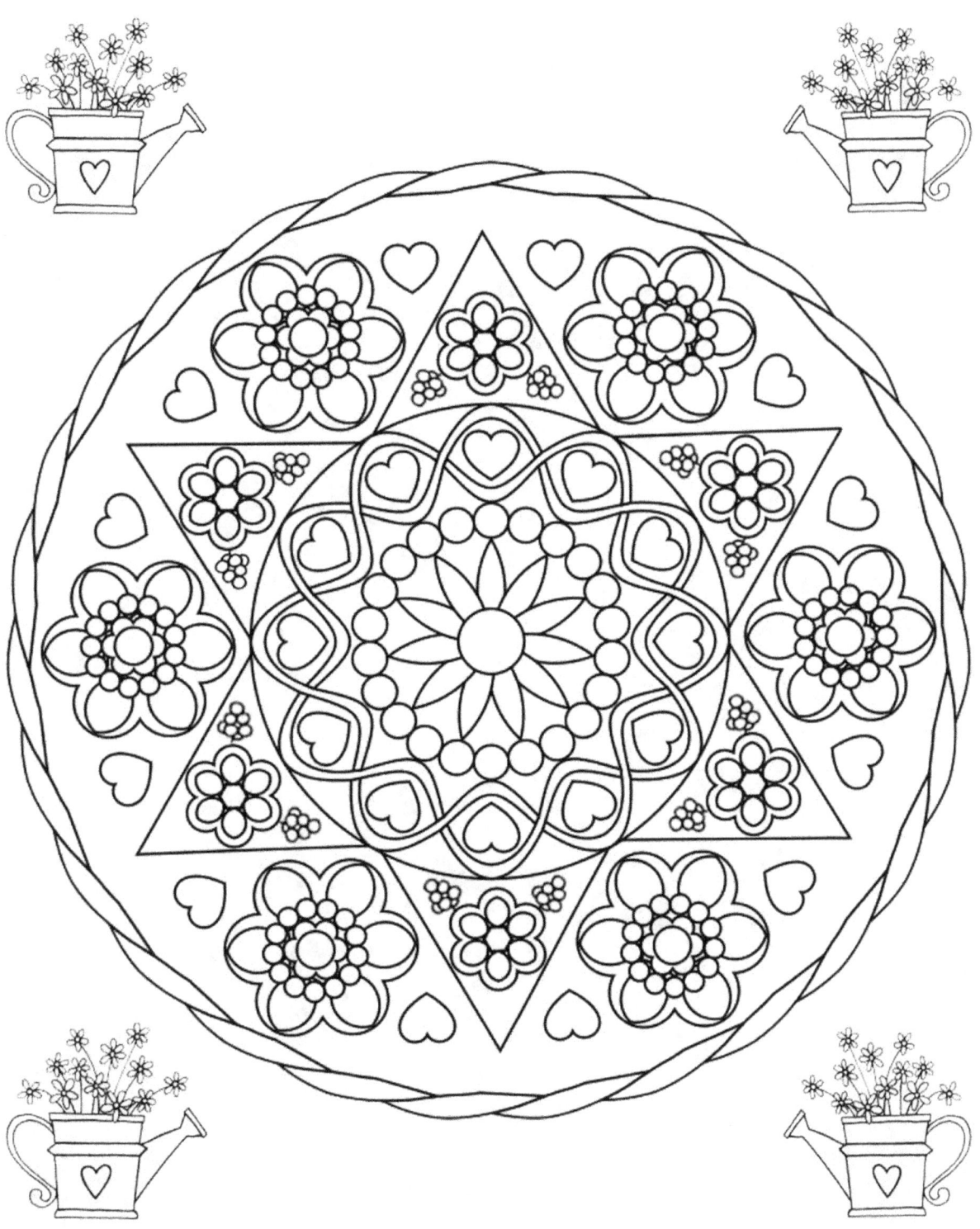

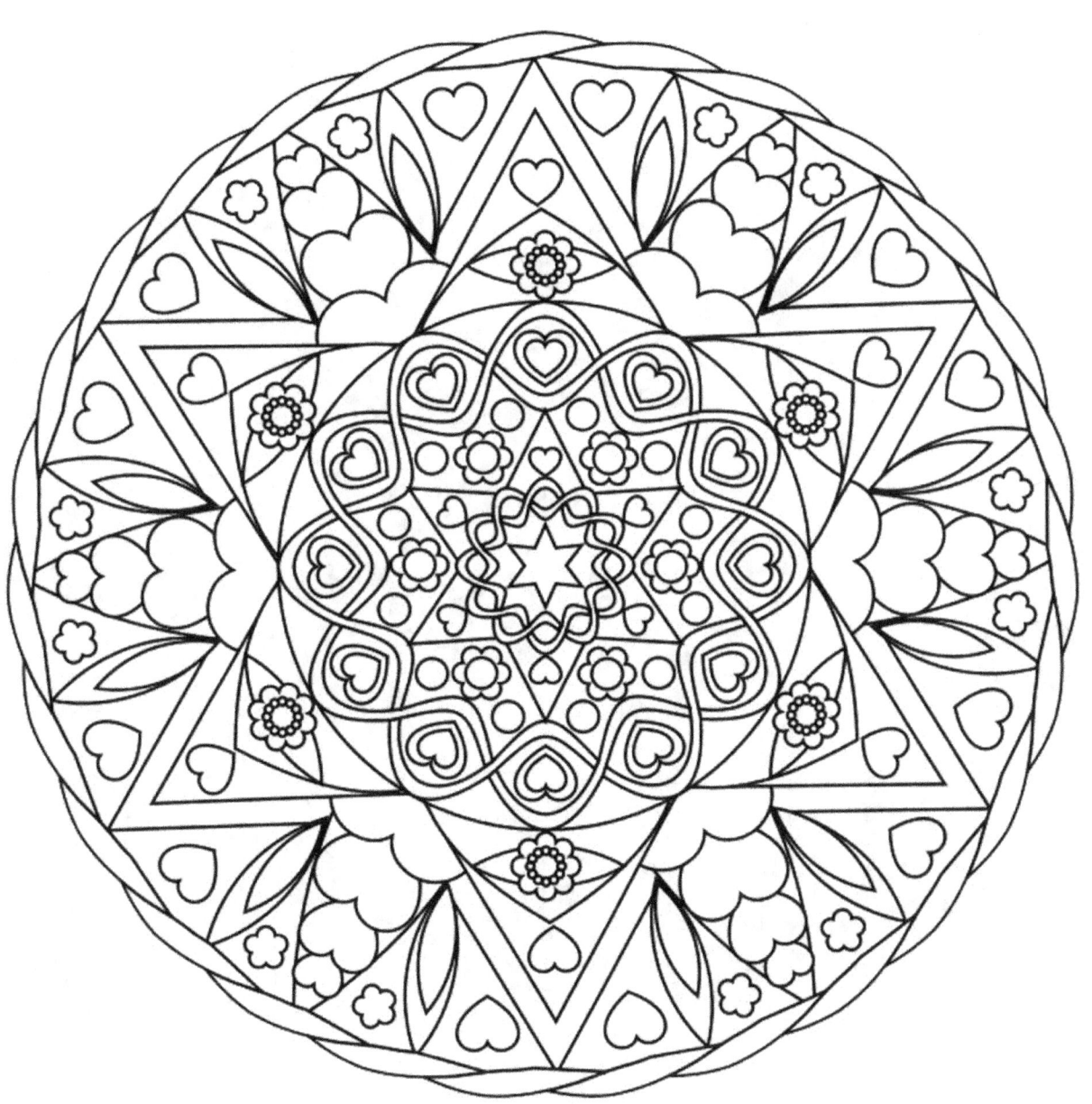

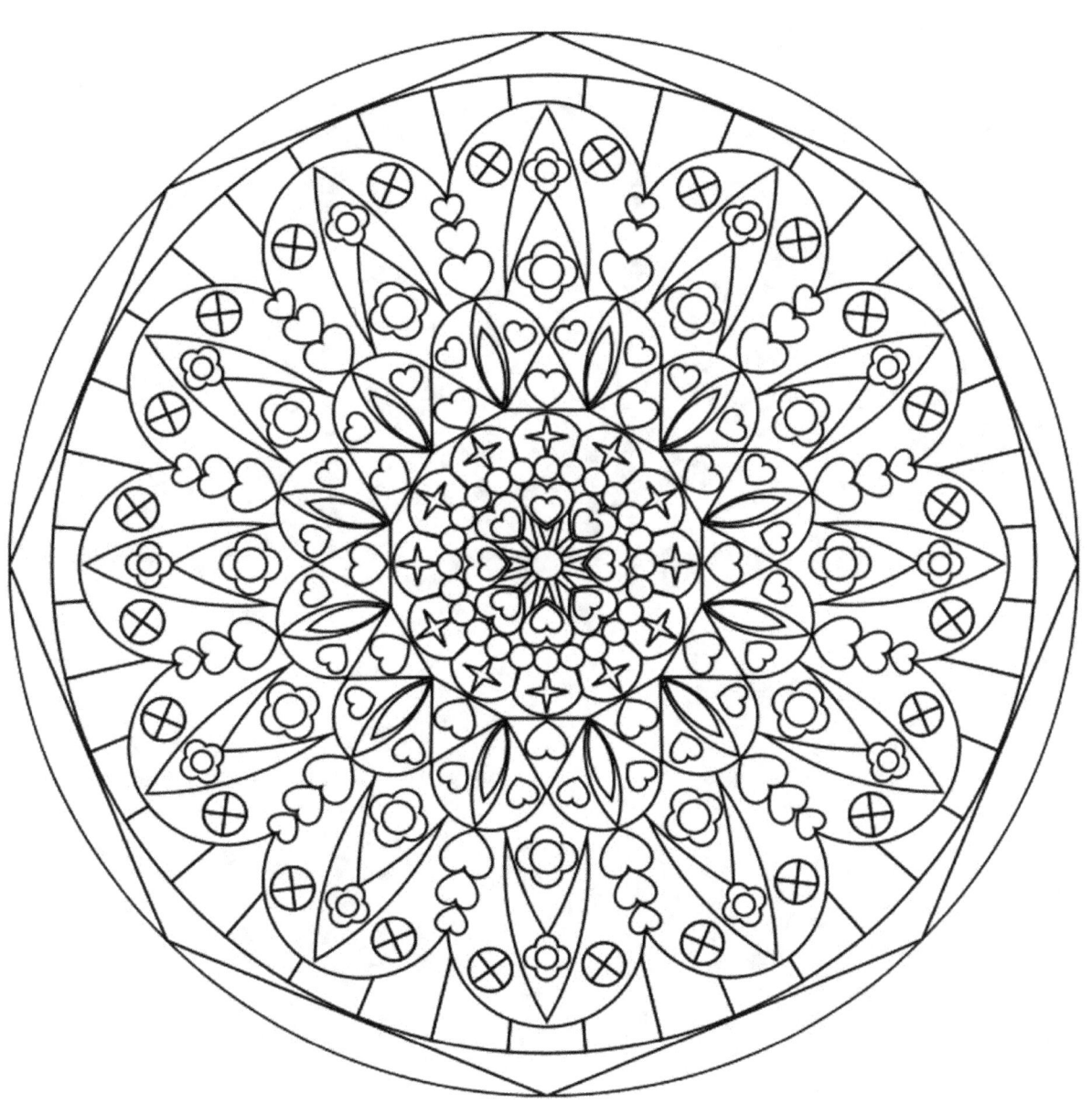

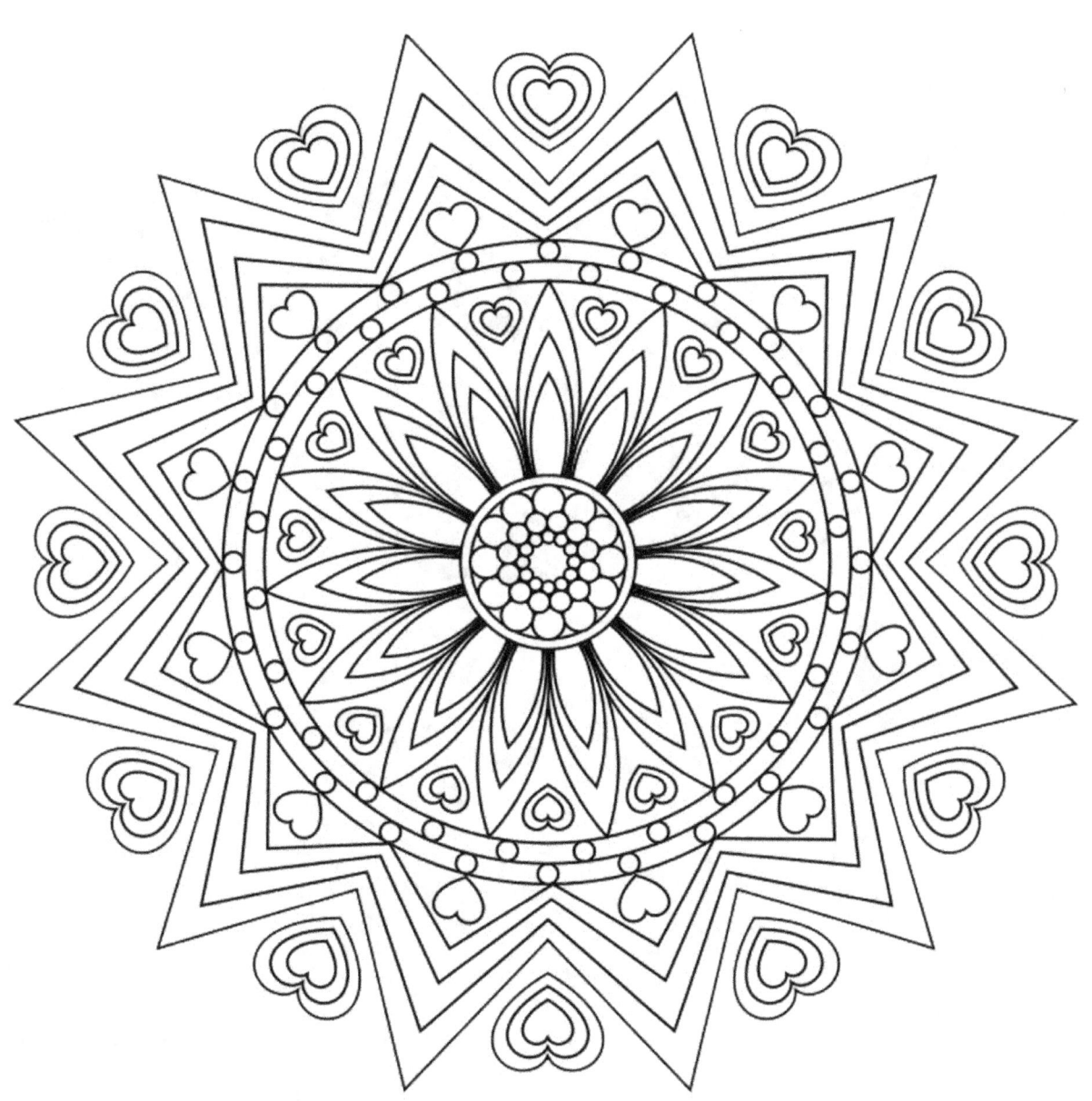

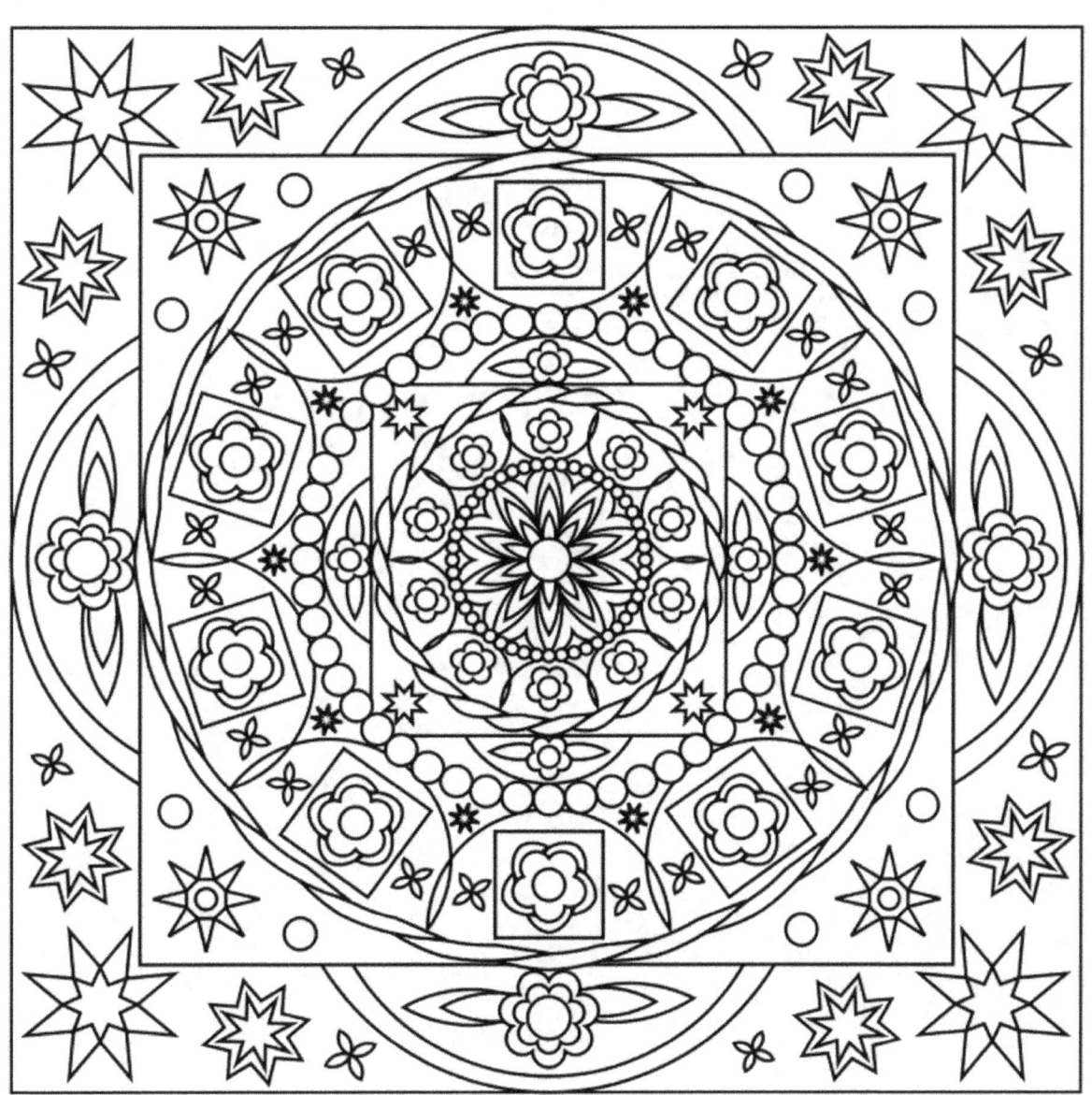

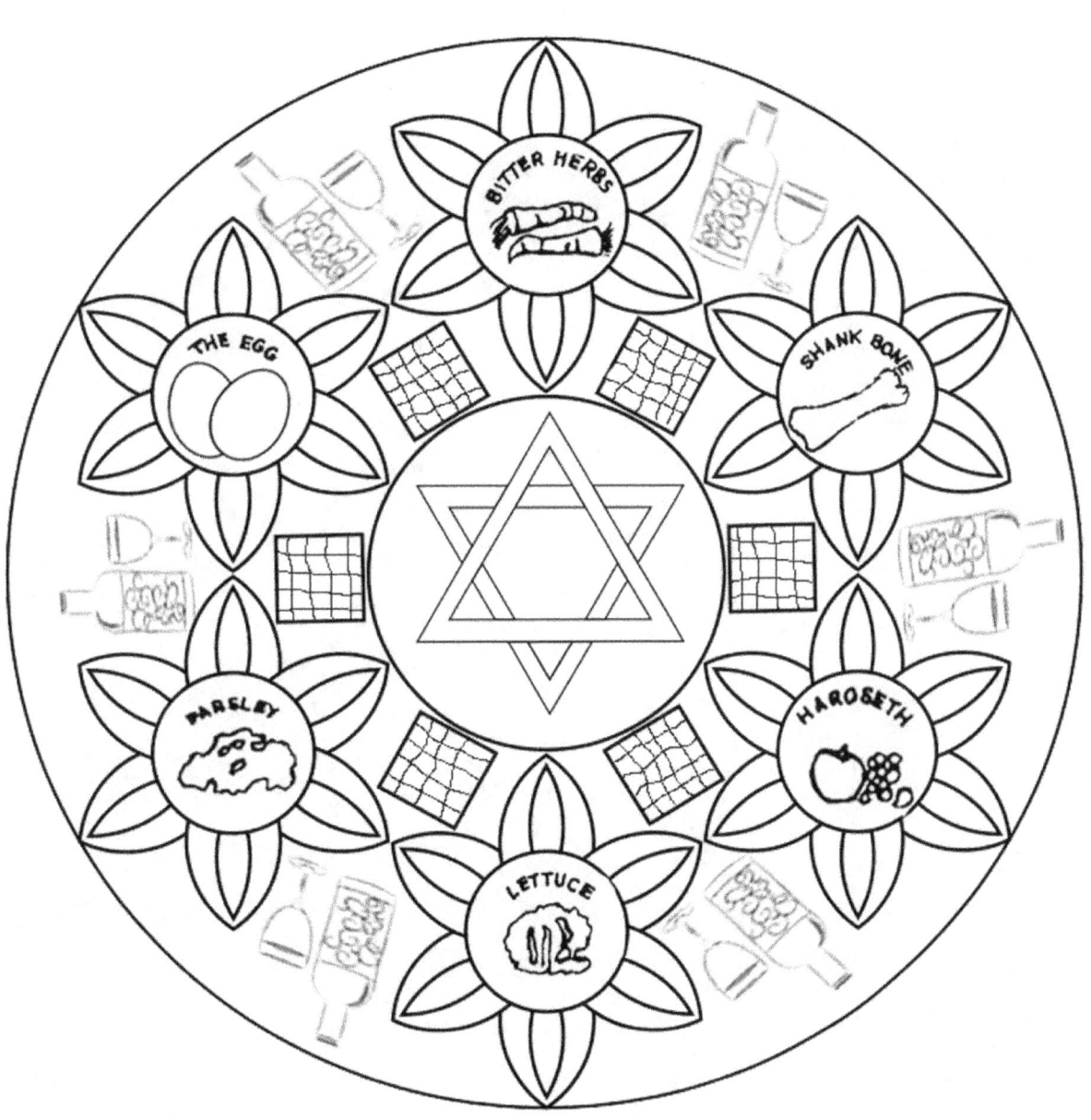

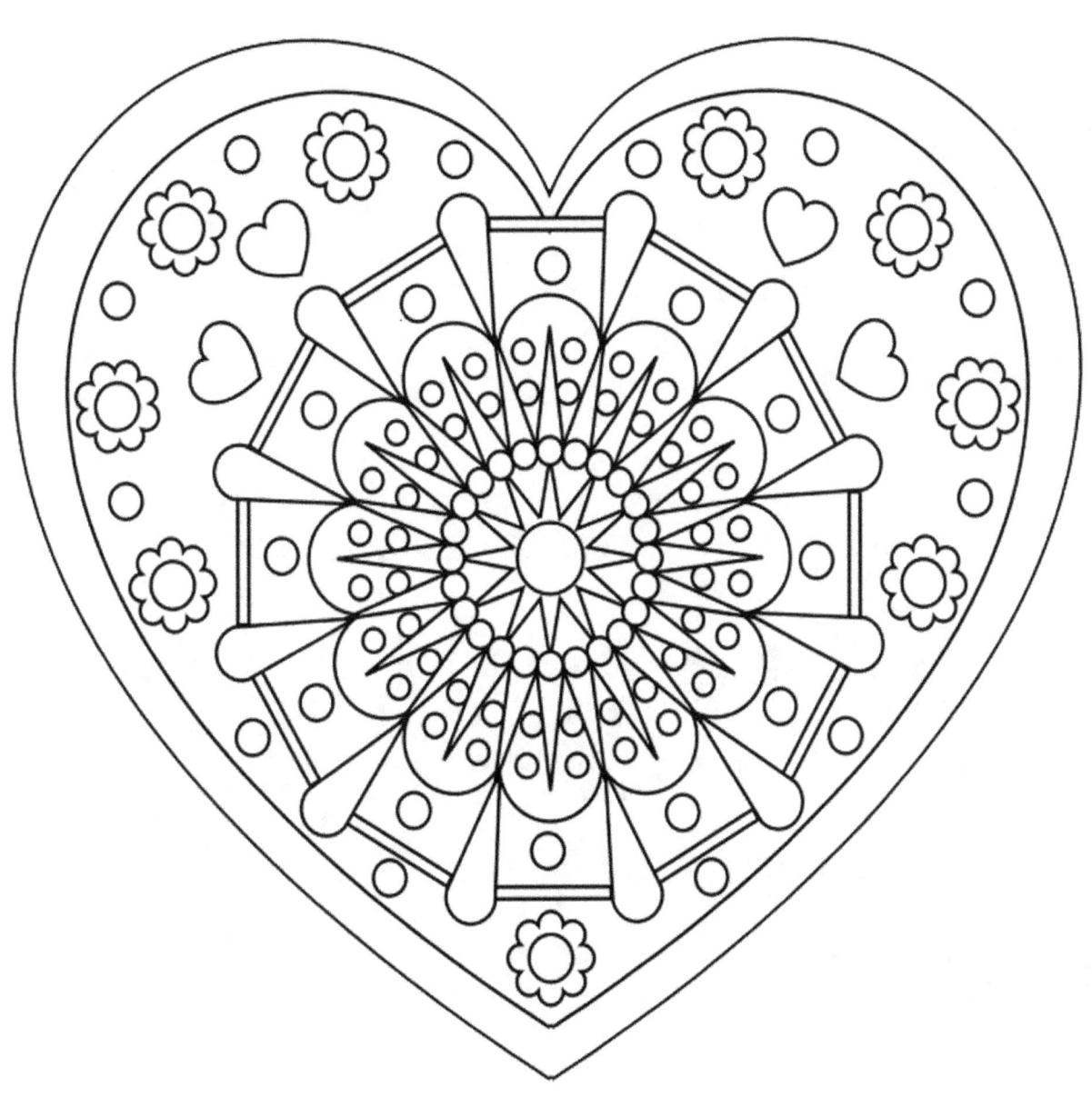

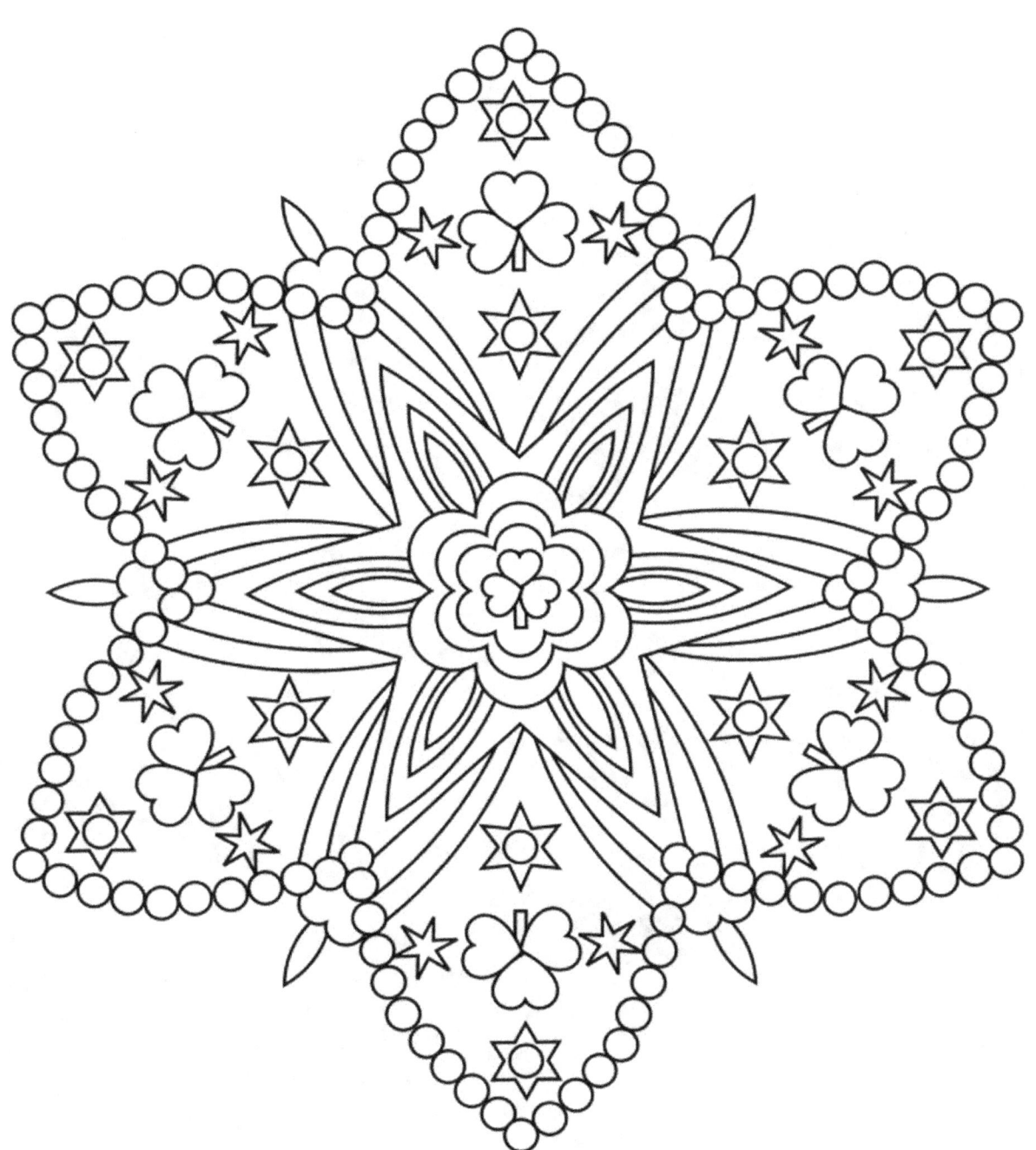

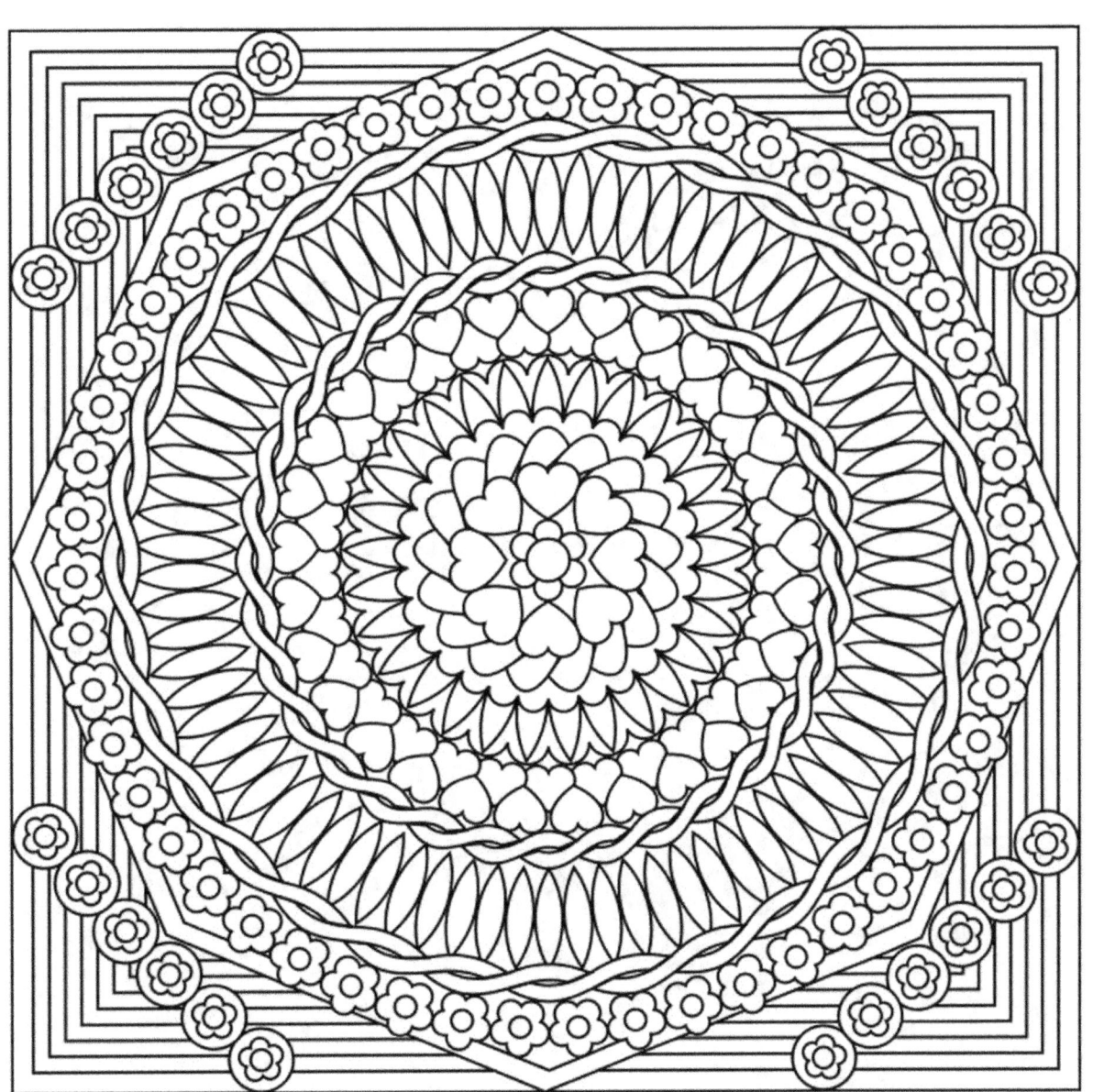

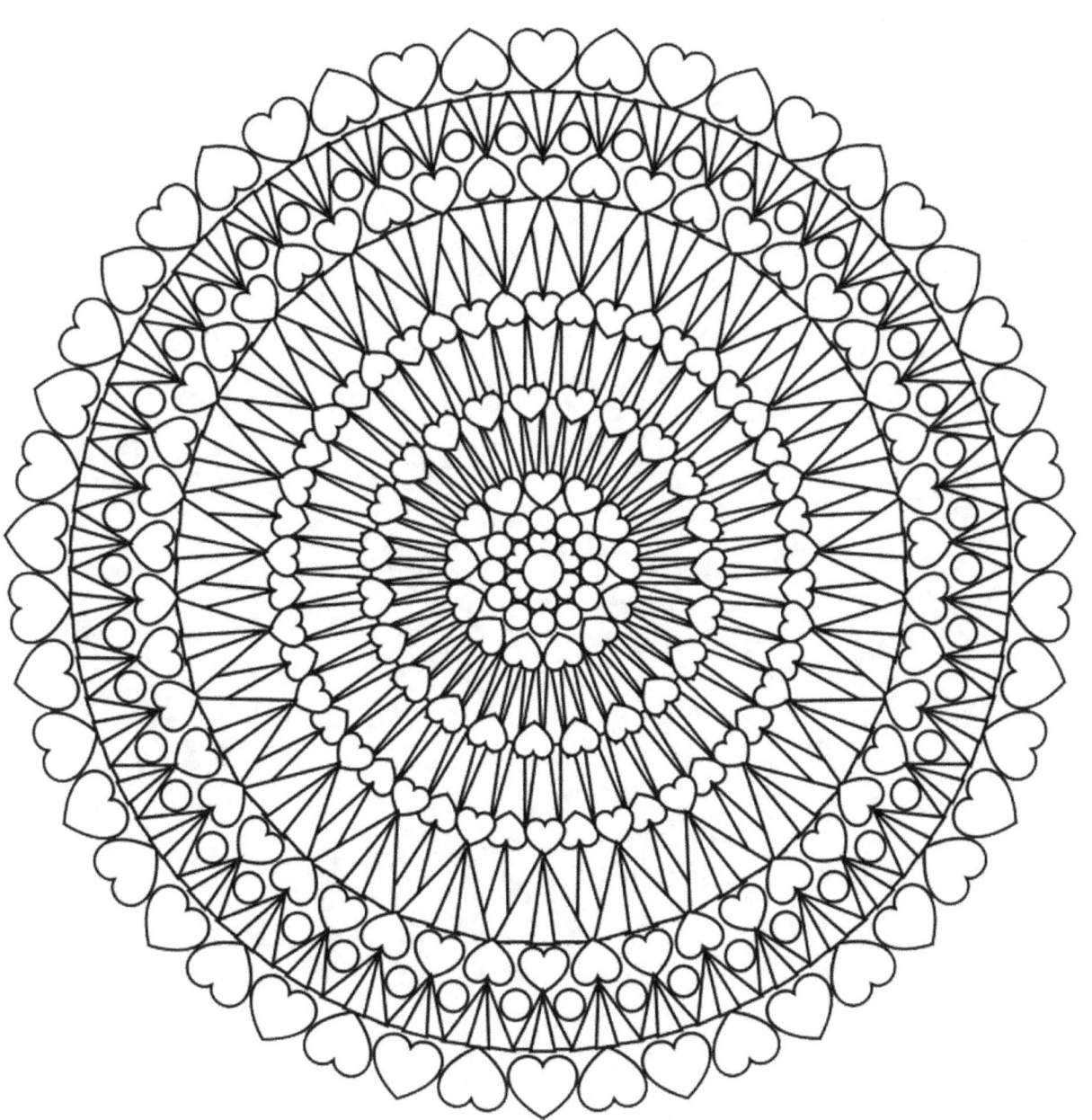

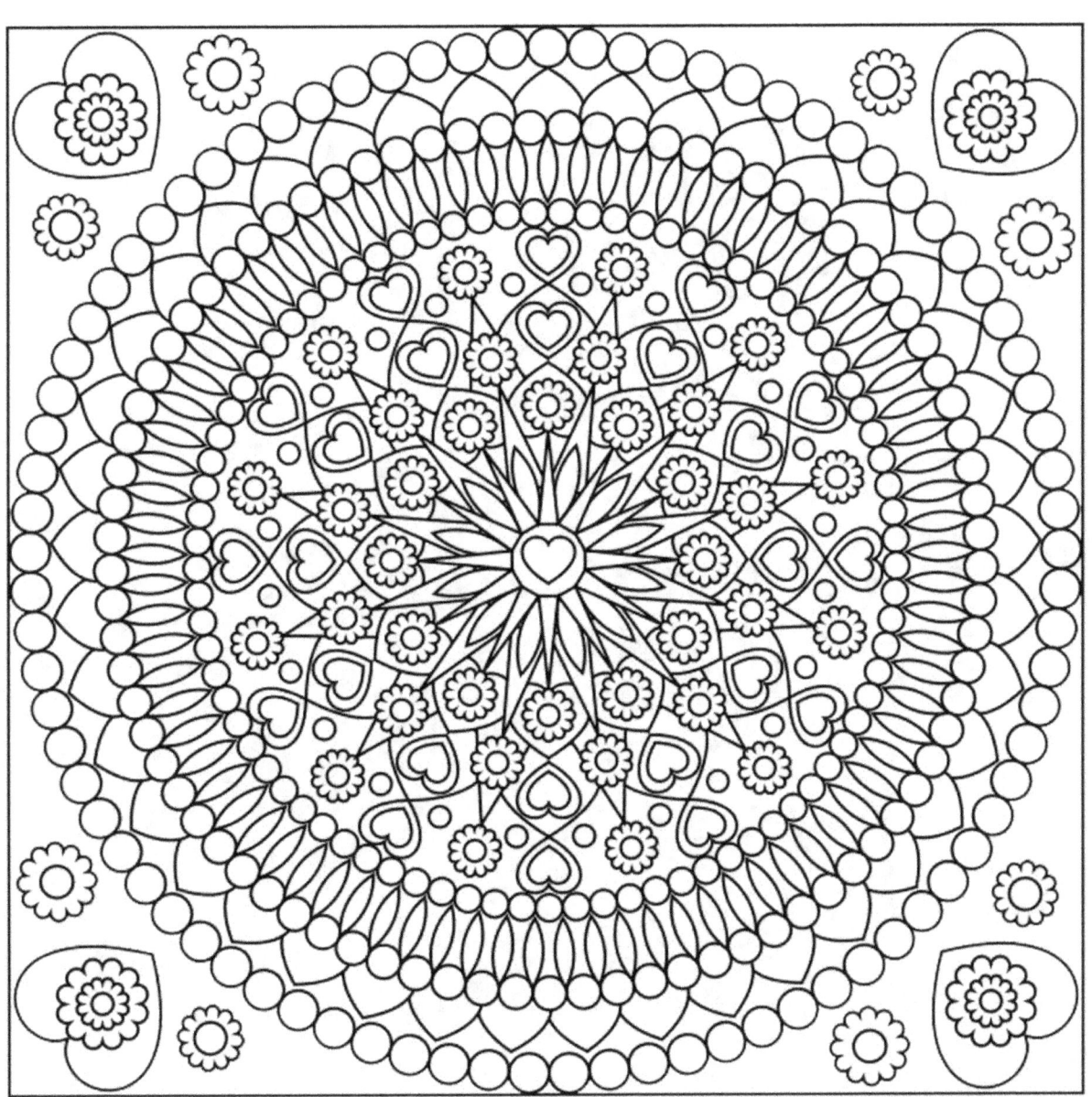

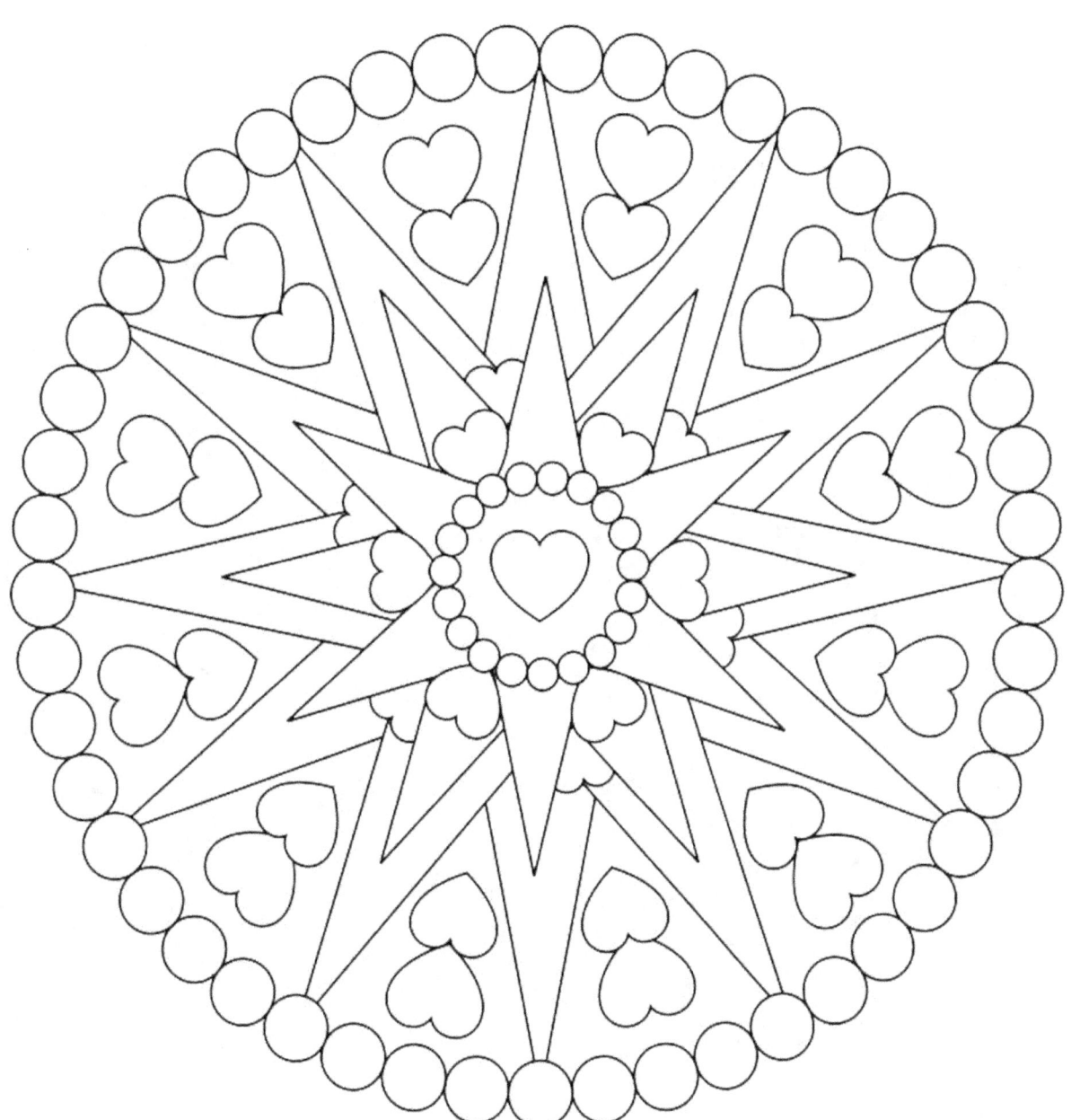

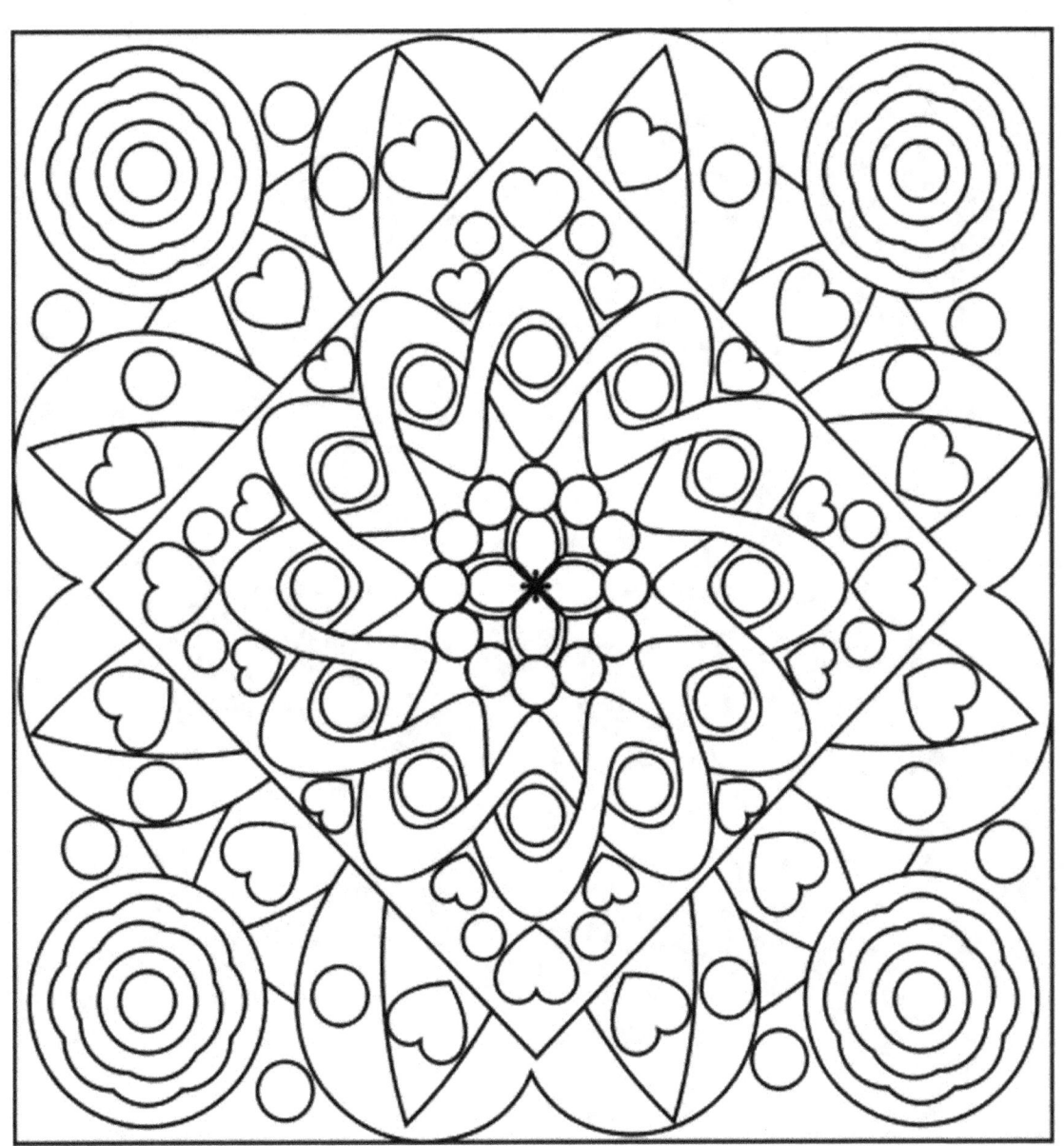

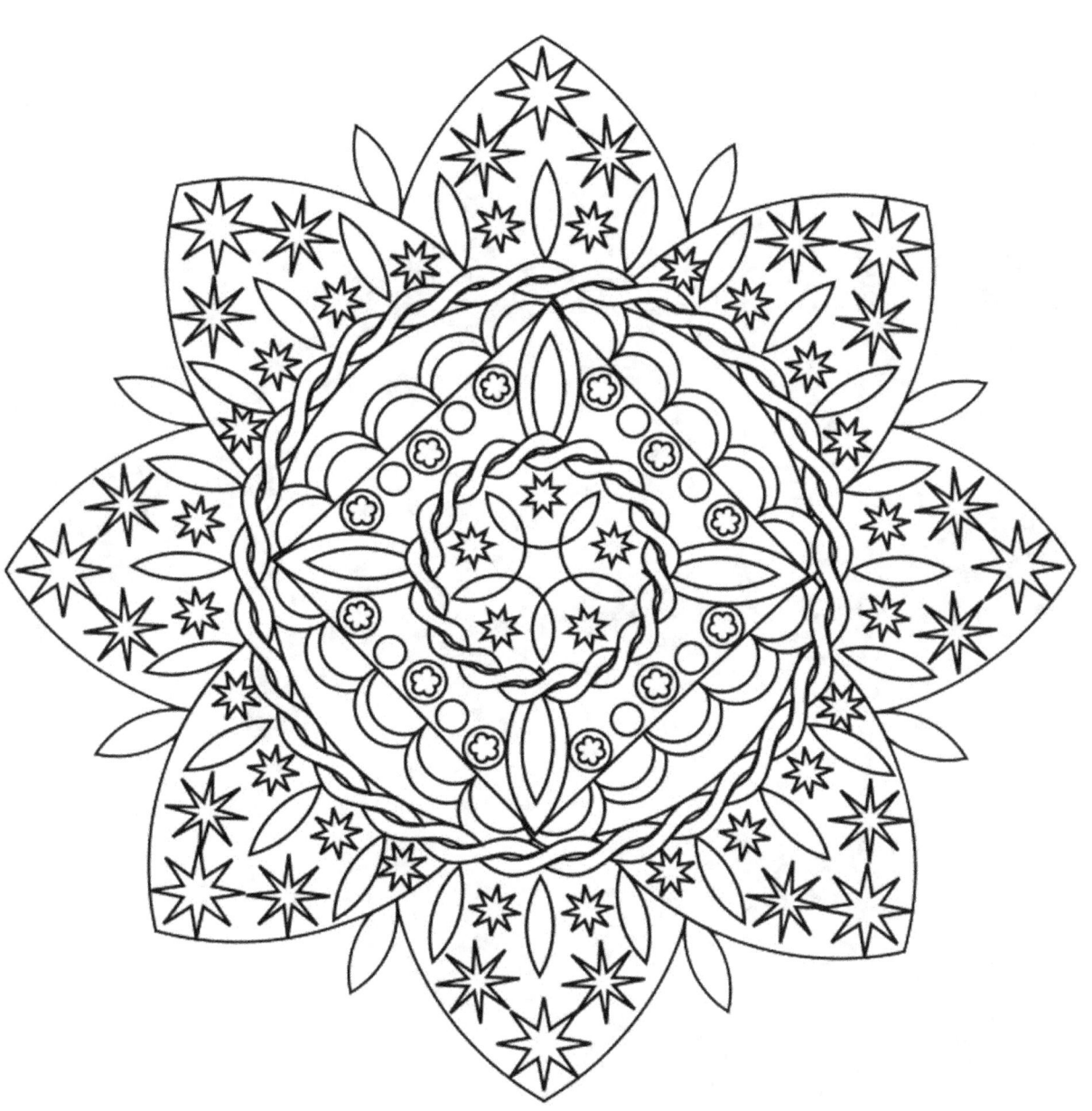

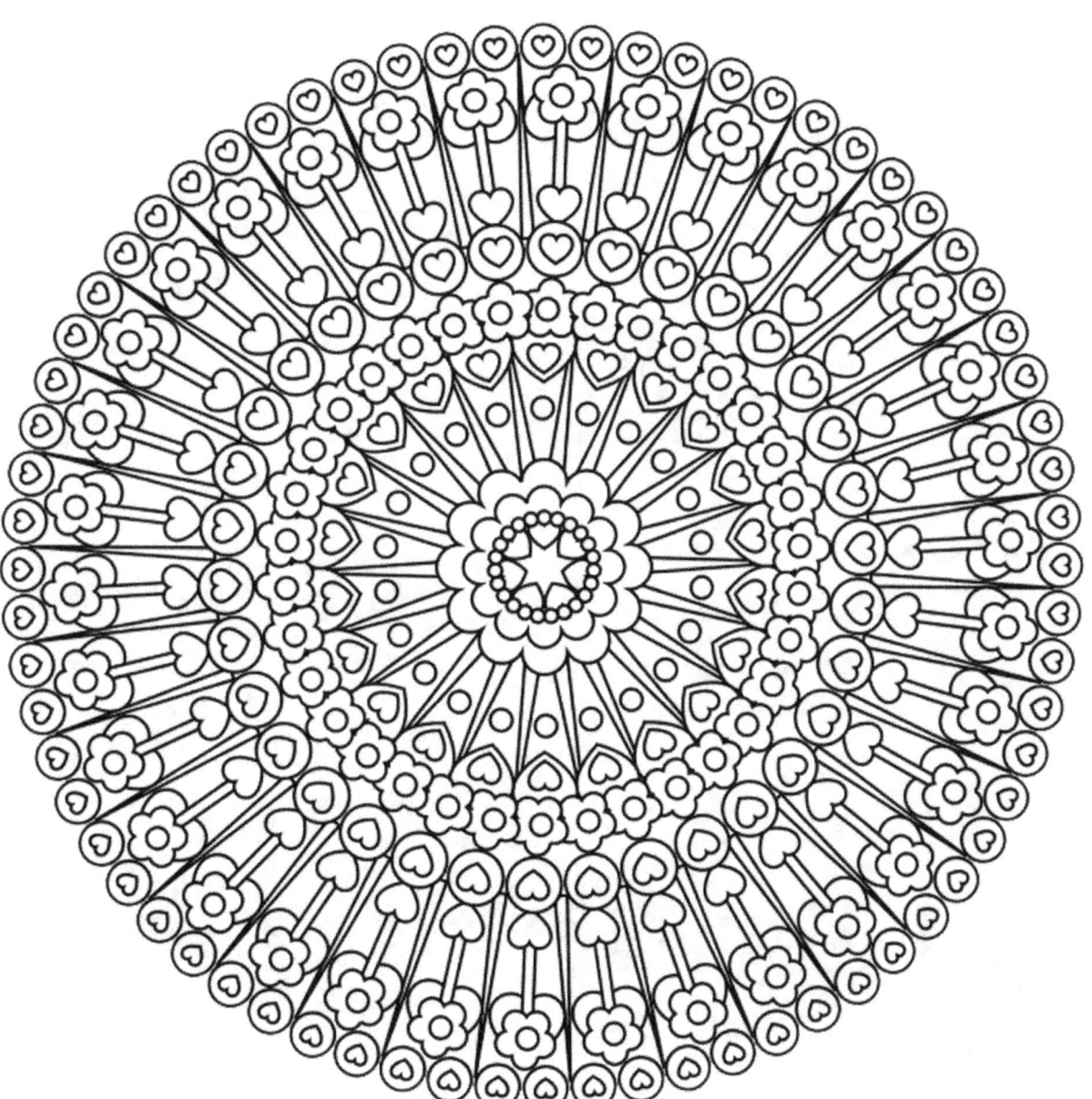

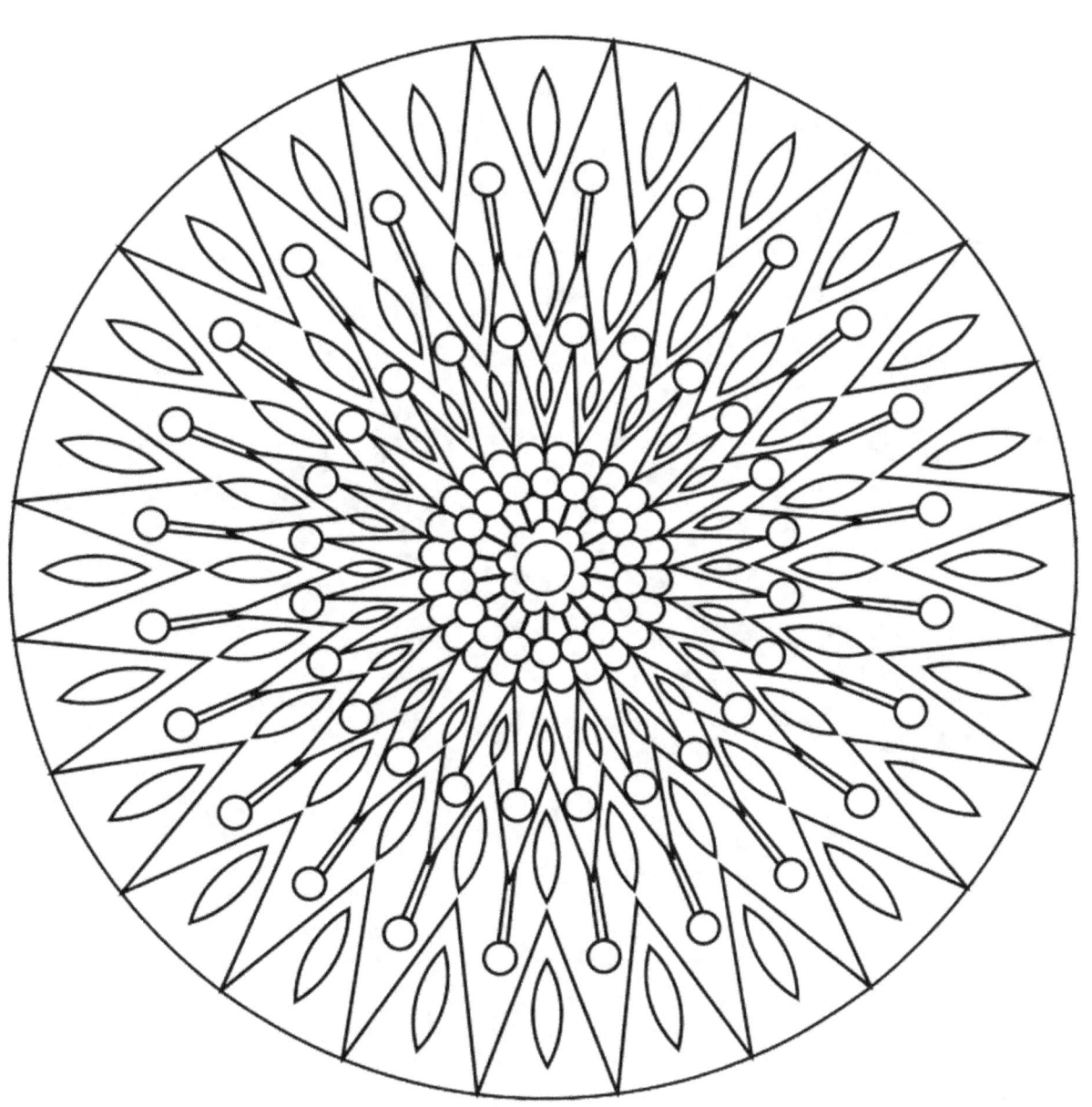